Moments that Take Your Breath Away

A fifth collection of prose & poetry

by Howard D Richards

Also, by Howard D Richards

Snapshots in Time 1, (2014)
Brief Encounters, (2015)
Snapshots in Time 2, (2015)
Romania, (2016)
Greece, (2016)
Snapshots in Time 3, (2017)
Islands of the Tyrrhenian Sea, (2017)
Snapshots in Time 4, (2018)
Adventures in Turkey, (2018)
Travels through Italy, (2018)
A short Collection of prose and Poetry, (2018) and
updated are Interesting Times (2020)
Blue Remembered Hills, a second collection of prose &
poetry (2020)
Arcady Lost or Found?, a third collection of prose and
poetry (2020)
Times They're a Changin, a fourth collection of prose and
poetry (2021)

ISBN : 9798846953222
Imprint: Independently published

To all those that are working to solve the effects of climate change and conjure solutions for human pandemics

.

Howard D Richards August 2022

"Poetry is emotion put into measure. The emotion must come by nature, but the measure can be acquired by art."

Thomas Hardy

"Real generosity towards the future lies in giving all to the present."

Albert Camus

"One cannot and must not try to erase the past merely because it does not fit the present."

Golda Meir

The covid pandemic and the adverse effects of climate change has taught us new ways of living and appreciation of what nature and the Earth has to offer.

Howard D Richards

July 2021

Chapter 1: Poetry

"Poetry lifts the veil from the hidden beauty of the world, and makes familiar objects be as if they were not familiar."

Percy Bysshe Shelley

"Poetry is the spontaneous overflow of powerful feelings: it takes its origin from emotion recollected in tranquillity."

William Wordsworth

My poetry flows from experiences as time flows and from memories and the state of the world. Conflicts with reality and truth happen many times thus my poetry explodes, or diminishes, as a consequence.

Love Won't Fade Away

Lush green grass to lie on,

Sounds of distant cowbells,

Cast aside pink chiffon,

Romantic love here dwells

Shadows from nearby trees

Cast glittering splendour

From sparkling light of breeze,

Subtly highlights gender

Leaves rustling with zephyrs

Balance other motions

Of their true endeavours

Expressing devotions

The afternoon goes by,

Lovers now sated,

Reddish glow in the sky,

Desires liberated

Darker cool shadows form,

Look up, fully dressed,

To see heavens transform

Evening colours expressed

Emotional feelings

Ending a sublime day

Thankful for many things,

Love will not fade away

So much to Remember

For Thelma's Birthday 2021

So much to remember,

Those happy days.

In dreamland can travel back in my mind,

Swirling poetic images, warmed heart strings,

Reminding me when lives entwined

And those warm heady summers wandering.

Loving always,

Like a glowing ember.

Memories of Yesteryear
For Cicely's Birthday 2021

I sit and read, or travel in time by dreams

Resting on dunes, or by imaginary streams

So many memories of yesteryear

The woodland glades, glorious butterflies,

Wild flowers in meadows, - jewels of the alps,

And high mountains baring their icy scalps;

Cities too, history and fine art, are highs

And the canals of Venice bring a tear,

As well as exploring a new frontier,

Not forgetting the sea and sapphire skies

Travelling Dreams

Down winding lanes, across hillsides,

Lush with vegetation,

To where a high mountain divides,

By imagination

Beyond the col see wooded land

With isolated hills

And in far distance sea and sand

Dreams that desire fulfils

Skim green treetops, racing shadows,

Drifting with warming wind.

Over rocky outcrops, time slows

For to a hilltop pinned

Here float amongst blown wild flowers

And scents of thyme and sage,

That have exceptional powers

Forcing mind to engage

Remembering, before moving on

The beauty and pleasure.

Now range over a paragon

Wandering at leisure

Over roofs of village houses,

Orange terracotta,

And honeyed limestone walls rouses

An image sonata

Speed over scattered villages

Amongst forested hills

To far blue mountain images

Their looming presence thrills

Enchanting blackberry highlands

Beyond the azure blue sea,

Ridges where Aleppo Pine stands

And slopes with tumbling scree

Zoom to Massif de l'Esterel,

Rugged and deep ravines,

Bare slopes where hot red rocks excel

And oak appealing greens

East along the Riviera

St Raphael to Cannes

To Juan les Pins to Antibes,

And over promenade of Cagnes

See fishermen with boats and net

That men pull from the shore

I stop to see what catch they get

And hear their fruitful roar

Go down to a rough sandy beach

To lie under the sun,

Water gently laps, hear faint speech,

And others having fun

But return from dreams with a start,

half remembering,

Strings still tugging at my heart,

Awake from slumbering

Timely Godsend

Catastrophic climate change is with us,

Sea level rises, forest fires, starvation,

As global weather changes for the worse

Through our atmospheric warming curse.

Will COP 26 be our salvation?

The world is far from harmonious,

And at times very acrimonious,

So can't have realistic expectation

- We will blunder on until the end

With population and media clamour

With moments of political madness

And old sages expressing their sadness,

But scientist and engineer endeavour

Will turn out to be a timely godsend

Providing working solutions that transcend

That humanity has to thank forever

Afghan Civil War

Young Afghan children scream and cry,

We ask ourselves oh why, oh why

Mothers in burkas sit quietly

Hiding oppressed humanity

Through actions of extreme bigots

Forcing a Muslim ersatz

Chaos and civil war rages

With return to Middle Ages

Through the wild fiery Taliban

With Sharia law in the can

As the country is overrun,

They clamp down on learning and fun

A crude misogyny unfurls,

No education for girls

Taliban

The population it mistreats,

No music allowed in the streets

Cutting off hands and put out eyes,

And stoning to death their prize

How many will die in the streets

Or of starvation with faint bleats

This is a problem for Muslims to sort

Where is Turkey, Saudi Arabia,

Iran, Pakistan and others to thwart.

Que esto no es labia.

Northern France

Through country lanes and roads of northern France

Some straight as a ruler, tree lined for shade,

Others winding through grass strewn wild flowers,

Where blue chicory lights up dark bowers

And stands of oak nestle in a cool glade,

Such mesmerising beauty in a magical trance,

Only by wandering backwaters perchance,

An ideal landscape for our pleasure made

Pass through sleepy villages made of stone,

Others timber framed buildings brown and white,

Over hump-backed bridges crossing bright streams,

The waters green from vegetation gleams.

Picnic in verdant forest to delight

With paté and baguette in a place unknown

Until we ventured in to this lush green zone

Where in the thick woodland might be a sprite

Woke sleepily from our pleasant repast

To move onward to a provincial ville

The quiet wood cool in the hot afternoon

But soon to insect noises, ears attune

The road leads to a hotel for a traveller,

A small Logis, expectant for our foie gras,

With wine from Bordeaux in a cut glass,

That has moisture running from the chiller

Later enjoyed dinner that Madame cooked,

A fried trout vinaigrette served with fresh bread

Followed by petite pois a la Francaise

It was a fine meal fit for a gourmet.

No dessert, settled for cognac instead

With coffee and chocolate mints nicely wrapped

That we enjoyed at leisure, over stuffed,

Before going unsteadily to bed

When will the Sun Shine on Afghanistan?

When will the sun truly shine on Afghanistan,

When will all its people feel free,

When will men and all the women be equal,

Free from the Islam yoke they plea

A country in instability and chaos,

Intruders from other states,

The world of Islam forcing worst messages,

Those oppressive religious fates

Ethnicity a core problem causes crises,

Pashtun have too much influence,

Hot bed of Sunni Muslims and Pakistanis

Dangerous region that takes offence

When State doesn't run religion

And all races are accepted

Men and women will have no fear,

For people will be respected

To do this expel all bigots,

Have tolerant society,

Become true Afghan patriots,

And upbeat with variety

Refugees Refuge from Hell

In the chaos of twenty-twenty-one

An Afghan family was brought to England

And settled in fine Sheffield in a hotel.

Alas, a son of five to his death fell

Their dreamland from Kabul shattered and dammed.

No true health and safety inspection done,

Why so careless for the family's freedom won,

Those responsible should be shammed and slammed

The little boy fell from the high ninth floor

To his mother's pitiful screams and anguish

A saddened body with blood and gore

What do the Afghans think of the British?

Wrapped in Melodrama

Out of Afghanistan in chaos,

Guilty in the ultimate panic,

Children killed by Americans

By great dishonour that is Man's.

The President's face, sardonic,

Recalling Vietnam and Laos.

Those left behind was it pathos?

Unknowns ahead, melodramatic

Lifting the Spirit

That meld of yellows, oranges to reds

Late bright summer colours through to late fall,

In which lavender blues to purple threads

Flowers like crocosmia and echinacea enthral

Though there are many other flowers to see,

Swept back helenium, rudbeckia

And sublime kniphofia to name three,

But not forgetting alstroemeria

Then the leaves and specially the trees

Oaks, Beeches and highly varied maples

Become the magnificent stars to please,

As deciduous woodland mainstream staples

Yet mustn't forget those strong blueish threads

Some discrete, hidden away, as gentians,

A bold symphony of asters in beds,

Not forgetting those blue geraniums

But it is the golden glow of autumn

That warms the heart and lifts the spirit

And brightens in a woodland's foggy bottom

- That annually we all inherit

Extinctions

How much have we lost?

Those wild flower meadows,

Butterflies galore,

Bird life and much more.

Air around now shows,

Insects, at what cost?

Farming holocaust,

So many, who knows

It's not just insects

It is mammals too

And all the fishes,

Kelp and seagrasses,

All ocean milieu.

Industry effects,

Do we have regrets?

Man turning the screw.

Then there's the world's trees,

Lost variety,

Through forest burning,

For farming and mining,

Man's impropriety,

As well as disease

And climate's unease,

Intense anxiety

Ancient Venetian Bridges

Within a thick wooded valley, in Cyprus,

lie medieval Venetian bridges,

Along a trail that crosses the high Troodos,

For caravans with commercial pledges

Now these old historical vestiges

Are hidden away by thick foliage

In the deep river ways subterfuges

That you need to seek out their heritage

Their wondrous curved arches in brick or stone

Place man's presence in the silvan landscape

Along ancient trackways that are moss grown

To a realm in which there is no escape

New Foundations

A slick return of summer, in high twenties,

Leaving behind those cool dreary grey skies,

A respite from climate realities,

Its seductive cadences mesmerise

An overture to an idyllic fall,

Lazy days amongst late garden flowers

With many shades of green leaves before the call

To ochres and reds in golden hours

An Indian Summer of times passed by,

Where the countryside expresses its flair

After harvests gathered in, beatify,

Changing the colour palette, with a fanfare

At ease contented and happy with life

Warmed by the sun, bathed by the serene moon

Leaving behind any signs of inner strife

Seasonal seductiveness not immune

Building up strength to survive dark winter days,

Recharging batteries through florid sensations.

This is our world to enjoy through hidden ways.

That we need to pursue with new foundations

Destroyer of Worlds

Sitting, thinking

The world's no longer what it was,

Too many humans,

Facing destruction to their own ends,

An anarchy,

Relying on religion and shibboleths,

Populist cults,

The meaningless of celebrity,

Inane creatures,

What a pitiful waste of aliveness

Sustain beauty

The simple pleasures of landscape and sea

Awesome mountains,

The variety of flora and fauna,

Feelings of grandeur

Knowing that you are always part of this

Not worthless,

But an intellectual being

Use it wisely,

Or be a potent destroyer of world's

Wartime Tearaways

Feel the heat, the scratchy grasses,

Pushing through dust clouds from parched soil,

Lines of dirty runnels of sweat,

Eyes sore from blinding light onset,

The gang in channels onward toil

Progress as afternoon passes

See what the lie of the land is,

Careful, mustn't the surprise spoil

Leap and charge with yells and loud screams

Fighting the other gang, tumbling,

Suddenly over with laughter,

The fear and challenge sort after,

Now in the fine grasses rolling

Happy days, all not what it seems.

Kids in wartime did what it deems

Little control, pretend playing

Fathers absent, mothers working,

Out of school a world of delight

Passions of youth, creative play

A world of dares and quandary,

Excitement at an air crash site,

Were tearaways, sometimes fighting,

Often tunnelling and exploring,

Ending at chip shop, late at night

Pleasure Seeker

Grey-white mist within the valley

Filters and diffuses sunlight,

That orange-yellow flowers glow

While pinkish-purples more muted.

All remains still and secluded

Beside bright silky webbed meadow

In the olden village hollow.

Stone houses in brightening light

Sleepy still, except for Sally

Who runs along the quiet road

Pony tail swinging, striding out,

Enjoying morning exercise

Under the opening clearing skies

Not far from her homely abode

Of her beauty she has no doubt,

Taking pleasure from her skin tights

Soaking up her youthful delights

A Poem for Maureen's Birthday

Just a tiny little drink on your birthday.

Celebrate changing colours that autumn brings.

Be happy, - watching the leaf fall ballet,

It's one of nature's truly pleasant things

Look at those flowers the pinkish-red Nerines

See the beauty in the form that you admire

To bring you joy more than any other means

And those extraordinary insights that inspire

U3A Walkers

Walking with the U3A once more,

A happy band plodding slowly ahead

Across meadow grasses, through ploughed straw,

By woodlands and along canals in awe

Of adorned narrow boats, as we tread,

Reading their novel names with flair galore,

Then back to country routes since days of yore,

Overgrown with nettles and brambles spread

Joys of pushing through avoiding root trips

Getting scratched and stung, clay sticking to boots,

All this taken in stride of seasoned walkers,

Cool and unfazed the social talkers,

Fortitude, tolerance, their attributes,

Ultimate goal focused on beer foamed lips

And perhaps a lunch of fish and chips

At a welcome inn of good reputes

Waiting the Beating of the Drum

Cooler winds from northwest blow in,

Swirling leaves along country lanes,

Raising goose pimples on my skin,

Facing up to autumnal pains

When gloomy days herald winter,

Those dark depressing days to come

Waiting for dreamworld to enter

And magic of Christmas for some

Who knows what the next year will bring?

There're many challenges for man,

How many birds in spring will sing?

Must solve climate change, if we can

Humanity now on the edge

Facing more tragedies to come

Scornful of, politicians pledge,

Waiting the beating of the drum

Wild Ragusa Rose

White sand, - feeling it run through my toes

Climbing a dune towards dark distant trees

Sheltered from the bright glare of midday sun.

Heavy going, - not easily done,

Legs dig deeper, getting there by degrees.

Peaked at marram grasses where wild wind blows,

And in amongst sprawling rugosa rose,

Sheltered from steadily increasing breeze

Many pink roses with fragrant flowers,

A delight to see amongst swishing grasses.

Purposely onward toward shade of pines,

Far out to sea storm clouds, ominous signs,

Hearing creaking sounds of disturbed branches.

In shadows looked out at building towers,

Soon cumulonimbus thunder showers

Fortunately, north west, in avalanches

Here the brilliant sun still burnt the sands,

Though cooler amongst dark green swaying pines,

Staring at nature's theatrical thrills,

Seeing lightening flash against blue-grey hills

Followed by noise like detonating mines,

As the tempest departs to distant lands.

Walk out across the dunes to silvery strands

Where the legendary red rose shines

Tall Grasses

Grasses blowing in wind, feathery light,

Sparkling in sunlight,

Through darker days tall and graceful as giants,

Winter defiance

Shelter as guardians until the spring,

There small insects cling,

Then cut down and trimmed for a new year's boom,

For flowering soon

For pollen to be carried on the wind

Certainly spellbind

With their ageing and maturing beauty

Waiting their duty

Spiders' Webs

Foggy days, ethereal mists,

Moisture gathers on spiders' webs,

Bright orbs, one of nature's true gifts

With strong fine silken silver threads

Seen in grasses, and shrubby sets

Creating gossamer displays,

Sometimes spooky, all tangled nets

That to the eyes truly amaze

It's an orchestrated vision

That fades with gentle warming air

Protecting the spiders' mission

That they can use their webs to snare

Tutu

Little Tutu at last arrived

My lovely bronze ballerina

With her dress and shoes shaded blue

An outstanding statue to view

With exceptional patina,

My inner spirit now revived

For she is much more than pint-sized,

- My little signorina

Angelic Paradigm

Baubles on the branches

Welcoming Christmas time.

Exhilarating snow

And Northern Lights aglow,

Angelic paradigm.

Take heavenly chances,

As moonlight advances,

The joy of pantomime

Christmas Dreams

Christmas through children's eyes is a magical brew,

Experiencing things beyond their imagination,

Yet love, excitement and enjoyment all comes through,

When growing up you lose such pleasurable sensation

Go back in time if you can, through conjured happy dreams,

See the wondrous enchanting world that time forgot,

Knowing that all imaginable is not what it seems.

There's something delightful in this place, but maybe not

Last Post

Autumn kniphofia and nerines

Brighten the garden's fading landscape

With magical scenes, far from has-been's,

Even though leaves falling as ticker-tape

Sycamore propellers cover ground

Aiming to germinate a forest,

But foiled by gardener's all the year round,

Eliminating them as promised

The Fall is that busy time of year

For tidying up and be put to bed

Hoping a sleepy hedgehog will appear

And snuggling over-wintering insects spread

Along the towpath from the Barley Mow,

Sky dark pewter, - passed by narrow boats moored,

Reached the aqueduct over Great Ouse flow,

As torrential rain had us truly floored

Left the other walkers to carry on

Along the soggy riverside meadows

Hiding their cares, seeing a lonesome swan,

Getting terribly wet from top to toes

We returned through down-pores, splashing through puddles,

Wetness penetrating, on through the gloom,

One of those unpleasant wet day struggles

Approaching eventual climate change doom

At last bedraggled back at the old inn,

Removing wet tops and muddy boots,

Trousers soaked to underclothes, - need a gin,

But drive home for coffee substitutes

46

Boscombe Down 1950's

I'm flying today

My grey coveralls on,

My high black boots too

And silk and leather gloves,

Carry my helmet

And my oxygen mask

Walk over the apron

To the waiting 'plane

Fighter or bomber,

I don't care.

Will do a series of tests,

May range widely to the Med

Before we're back to Boscombe Down

Post COP26

Politicians, as yet highly unwilling,

To take difficult decisions,

Humanity's destruction self-fulfilling,

For they have restrictive visions

They are too protective of their power

Not wanting to paint black pictures,

Wanting the same at the dark eleventh hour,

Solving economic pressures

Our world will descend into anarchy and chaos,

Shortages of food and water,

Living with humanity's profound pathos,

That will be too late to alter

And civilization will be destroyed,

Leaving small bands of survivors

Scratching a poorer living in the void

With no healthcare providers

Lucky to Meet You

Sixty years, seems like forever

How lucky I was to meet you,

My lover, My friend, My soul mate,

Now granddaughters to celebrate,

A sparkle in our dreams its true.

Encouraging them together,

The good times we will remember,

Shape the future let words imbue

I love you in many ways

Through our long autumnal days

Christmas Joy

In pandemic years look back to better times

When problems were not insurmountable,

The joy of Christmases like a poet's rhymes,

The unexpected highs redoubtable

Christmas tree lights and decorations,

Dressing up to nines and keeping warm,

Boxes of delights that fit expectations,

Our happiness and well-being transform

Christmas Tree

Walking the muddy country lanes,

Damp decaying vegetation

At depressing autumn's fag-end,

Towards the gloomy pinewoods wend,

Seeing with imagination

The fuller smaller spruce tree strains

For decorative Christmas campaigns

Creating a homely sensation

Taking back a favoured young tree

To plant within a Yuletide pot

And cover with baubles and lights,

Not forgetting those tinsel sights,

And the nutcracker man hotshot,

Before settling to evening tea,

Watching the twinkly lights with glee,

Thankful for the fine tree we got

Outside snow falls in large white flakes

Covering ground in a thick duvet,

Inside happy and contented

Knowing, Christmas not lamented,

Children wait to hear Santa's sleigh,

While mother bakes seasonal cakes,

And father works on cocktail shakes.

Perhaps will be like that again, someday

Fox in Winter

Cold, crispy snow on vegetation,

Brilliant in the moonlit starry night

All pale whiteness in the meadow,

With more sparkling frost to follow.

The waning yellow moon bright,

I look out with expectation.

In dark shadows, jubilation,

A foraging fox, to my delight

See pricked ears and elongated tail,

All bushy in the wintery hours,

Silently moving along the stream

Following scents to his secret dream,

Carefully around snowy towers,

But faster pulled by a well-marked trail

Through the village along the vale

Using his olfactory powers

Times when Young

So long ago it seems

Along by Ashmore Rails

Now only in my dreams,

As one of childhood's tales

Hiding from a steam train,

Excited by their sound

Not far from Blackhalf Lane,

Held in awe and spellbound

Then off to open rough ground,

Where slag heaps were overgrown,

And unsafe mine shafts abound,

Old workings left alone

Former individual digs

Covered by bramble patches

Looking like brier wigs

With sharp thorny catchers

Post war, without a care,

Building small hidden dens,

On the woody slag scarps

With my young gang of friends

Play for hours 'till sunset

When it was homeward bound,

Weary with some regret

And loudly fool around

Scruffily home at last,

Sent up to bath by mum,

As she saw me aghast

Smiled, yet was overcome

Later had my supper

And a bedtime story,

With a Horlicks cuppa,

Tuned to derring-do glory

Bird Feeders

Glad, birds on the feeders again,

Wild winter approaches,

Bringing icy cold it does pertain,

Seeing tits and finches

Other birds join the frenzy too,

Red robins and starlings,

A veritable motley crew,

With their comings and goings

I watch the seed level go down,

As the little birds get their share,

Pushing in on a starling clown,

Battling goldfinches have a flair

Like watching boisterous action,

Throughout a day it comes and goes,

These wild birds have an attraction

Helping them through the winter throes

Walks with the U3a

Assembling in all sorts of conditions,

A blissful band,

For one of the monthly walking missions,

The leader planned

Across the shire in pleasant neighbourhoods,

By footpaths and stiles,

Through villages, across fields, through green woods

Walking a few miles

Looking and seeing the unexpected,

Ridge and furrow,

Wildlife, botanical gems detected,

And Man's sorrow

Rubbish, farming destruction give concern,

But English landscapes

Inwardly please, for nature's glory yearn

Euphorically traipse

Over hills by hidden trails, see for leagues,

Along valley routes,

Such sensory pleasure serving all our needs,

Best of regions roots

Full of wellbeing arrive at an inn

To sup with pleasure

And to chat and laugh and dine within,

Life beyond measure

Longing for Freedom

My inner thoughts and visions curtailed,

In pandemic times.

Longing for full freedom to wander,

Exploring all.

Drifting through new historic landscapes,

Seeing with open eyes

All that remains melded in with insights

To a distant past

And to revel in the beauty as seen,

But finding ugly upsetting scars

From Man's industry.

Some in ruins, but others darkly stark

Causing inner outrage.

Greedy spoilers of the earthy world

In time will decay

And cover over with wild disorder,

A natural beauty,

A splendour surpassing man's desires.

Enchanting images,

Delightful and magical to dream upon

A Future Bright?

A cheerless pandemic winter,

Grey dismal skies,

Life goes on, but sometimes bitter,

Covid agonize

Is restricting social contact,

Broken families

Having severe mental impact,

Causalities

Enhanced by economic distress,

Many food banks,

Desperate hard times, with no Christmas largesse,

Enduring ranks

Brexit brought political tragedy,

Ruled by clowns

No understanding, - a travesty,

More close downs

The future could be bright with right leaders

Using knowledge,

With entrepreneurial stakeholders

With a goal pledge

What will twenty-twenty-two bring to us,

A glimmer of light?

Or more of the darkness with all the fuss?

Hope it is bright!

On the Road to Nowhere?

I'm walking the road to nowhere

Stuck in the gloom and woke madness,

The State's messed up, - I despair,

It's a time of great sadness

There are a few who could save us,

But only loonies are in charge

Supported by a populace,

Thoughtless and ignorant at large

Critical change a requirement,

From reactive to proactive,

Expertise at heart of government

That must be interactive

There are many challenges

For very long-term ambition,

And economic balances,

A new industrial mission

Many new ways of living,

Coping with climate changes,

Wasting time is unforgiving,

To overcome deadly dangers

Then be on the road to somewhere,

Where it's brighter and full of hope,

Not mindset of devil-may-care,

But solutions with plenty of scope

A Card from the Queen Today

We've got a card from the Queen today,

Wonder what it will say,

It's our sixtieth anniversary,

A memorable day

We've got a card from the Queen today

Unexpected delight,

A milestone in year of the Covid plight,

Enjoying it despite

We've got a card from the Queen today,

Full of gentility,

For your best wishes and cordiality,

Thank you, your majesty

New Year Blues

I'm suffering the new year's blues,

In the dismal days of winter.

The garden's drab and lacks colour

And grey skies couldn't be duller,

At times you look out and shiver.

As you look for things to amuse,

There's not enough to circumfuse,

So deep depression does linger

Boris's End?

Boris caught out with a big lie at last,

Interesting how Tories will wiggle out,

In their web of utter deceit held fast,

But in the end probably a cop out

The Media is having a field day,

Avoiding National and global issues,

Need PM's dismissal without delay,

And focus on economic values

To live better, dealing with climate change

And completely reform the health business,

Giving power to the people, not short change,

A strategy for UK's future wellness

Togetherness

Together in our autumnal years

Our love for each other persists

Enjoying our togetherness,

In many ways you can't express,

For it naturally exists

Like glow of celestial spheres,

Or feeling of happy tears

Wondrous Sight

Stroll in countryside on a fine spring day

Enjoy nature in its true glory time,

Bulbs and wild flowers in a cabaret,

Endlessly like catalytic ribozyme

Snowdrop, iris, crocus and hellebores

With early primrose, violets and daisies

And with catkins waving like semaphores

A truly wondrous sight that amazes

Winter Thoughts

Golden light on old limestone walls,

Sun blest, from winter's morning sky,

Darker shadows from bare branched trees

Dance delightfully in the breeze.

Balletic movements aurify,

Such theatre through the village calls,

Where fragile web of season falls.

A joy always I won't deny.

Blackbirds shuffling dead leaves for food,

Heads cock to one side to explore,

Yellow beaks grab their tasty finds,

Worms and insects of many kinds

And scurry on to find some more

Their instinctive desire renewed

Seeking with hope and fortitude.

Time spent watching them just adore.

The drab debris of winter garden

Awakened by bulbs emerging.

Brown remains to be cleared away

Readying for early spring's sway,

Tidying up and preparing

For an early blooming stardom

For winter's sunshine does embolden.

Tomorrow will find me willing

Brayfield to Denton

First ramble 2022

Under grey unpromising skies,

A landscape, all colour washed out,

Uninspiring views without doubt,

Only a monthly exercise,

Treat for January's debut,

Sticking to the others like glue

But knew would have to compromise

From Brayfield by worn grassy ways,

At times embellished with dog turd,

Through fields of tedious sameness,

Until reached sullen gloominess

Passed Solar farm on holidays

And passed gnarled trunks holding our gaze.

With quietness, only small talk heard

On towards Denton faced with mud,

Over a stile and to a gate

With sheep flock chasing towards me

And through the sucking mire carefree.

Walking on at a slower rate

To reach the main road to Bedford.

Left the others, knowing I should,

Because it was my agreed fate

Onwards by road to Red Lion pub

An undulating tiring slog,

Arriving in brighter Brayfield

To immense comfort that appealed.

Finally, now the epilogue

Drove home for drinks and grub

Aching limbs whittled down to nub,

Rambling days not a travelogue

Little Egrets

The egrets have arrived,

Three, fishing in the stream,

So many it surprised,

Their fine whiteness agleam

Firm and still on fences

Waiting chances to catch.

Using all their senses

Swiftly snatch and dispatch

After meal and preening

Roost in the tall maple,

Seen as restful perching

Like a ghostly candle

Until they all depart

In a flutter of white

Happy with the brook's carte,

To everyone's delight

Next day return to feed

And relax in the tree,

They are a blissful breed

Magical, wild and free

Churchill Wanabee

'Partygate' and Sue Gray

Boris in time will pay

For all lies and poor leadership

Costing the country billions

Must get rid of his stewardship

And follower reptilians

Need good proactive strategic government

To deal with climate change and new economy

To improve way of living and the environment,

Rebuff unruly schoolboy, Churchill wannabe

Snowdrops

Bright little Madeleines

In a small family group,

As snowdrop treasuries

With golden ovaries

Part of a larger troop,

Which are our pre spring friends,

With greenery that blends

And pale white heads that droop

Plicatus, Nivalis

And tall Elwesii

Delectable banquets,

Amongst snowy blankets,

With Woronowii

Dwell free from avarice

Yet so glamorous

In lucent patches lie

Future Prospects

Covid's on the wane we hope,

Two years lost to the virus,

When our hopes and ambitions

Were lost to other missions,

None overly desirous:

Buy through the lockdown did cope,

Extending our shopping scope

With outings to inspire us

Now promise of holidays

To our favourite places

And fast train trips for a start,

Civic culture and fine art,

Burst bubbles, see new faces,

Different things to amaze

Sitting with a dreamy gaze,

In those magical spaces

Desire full freedom again,

Experience all we want,

Life doesn't last forever

Catch up being together

Breakfast coffee and croissant

Watching people entertain,

Perhaps lunch of quiche Lorraine,

Blissful café bistro jaunt

An exciting time once more,

Through cities and countryside

Bathe with history and glamour,

Enchanting spots enamour,

Feeling senses amplified,

Body tingling to the core,

Lockdown was an utter bore

Now happy and overjoyed

Eunice

Eunice rages in with a blast,

Hitting the south of England hard,

More fuss than any Northern storm,

Which are much more of the norm.

Part of London centric regard.

Bulletins with concern broadcast

The North South divide have contrast

You cannot always disregard

Ukraine Invasion by Russia

Invasion by Russia of Ukraine,

Through mad megalomaniac Putin,

Has stirred up an emotional fervour

In the nation, to defend with valour,

Their freedom and democracy within,

Inspired by an obvious coup de main,

Say, we will stand and die, it's our domain,

Go tell Europe and NATO Putin's sin

Refugees pour across western borders,

Millions, mainly young kids and women,

Men eighteen to sixty stay and fight.

Zelinsky powerfully describes their plight

All resist in their so dark beginin'

Against mighty overpowering numbers,

With great bravery, battle aggressors,

But with many deaths in the end will win

Send safe journey to Zelinsky

Glory and freedom to Ukraine

Their extreme bravery no hyperbole,

Venture by Russia was insane

Shadows from The East

Grey shapes with children and oldies

Trudging on through shattered cities

Ruined by Russian bombardments,

Those escaping, the innocents.

Carry bags of few possessions,

Shell shocked, hollow faced impressions,

Disabled helped through rough terrain,

Elderly too at times of strain

Refugees find way to borders

By foot, car, train, from all quarters

And welcomed and looked after there

Before millions going elsewhere

The EU is a good haven,

Free from human mutilation

Yet other safe places needed

And their voices not unheeded

Those remaining women and men

Fight on bravely time and again,

Cities crumble in their domain,

Determined, faces showing strain

How much more bombing can they take

They persevere for Ukraine's sake

In the end their spirit will win

Counteracting Putin's grave sin

Lit-up Garden

Early sunlight on daffodils

Bright yellow turning with a breeze

Flaring long trumpets giving thrills

As Star of David petals please

Light up a gorgeous spring garden

And distract from darkness elsewhere

As war images just harden

With depravity in our glare

So beautiful the narcissi

Dancing gracefully in eyesight

Above green flowing waves so leafy

Amongst gold, starlit white so bright

Lighting Poignant Fires

Warm days, end of March,

Voices of blackbirds,

Songs from a tall larch,

No poetic words

Such beauty beyond expression,

Comfortable and happy times,

Away from Covid's depression,

And war in Ukraine, Russia's crimes

Walk down the river,

Trees bursting in bloom,

Emotional shiver

Gone winter's dark gloom

Joyful days of spring here again,

Nourishing the mind, feed desires,

A freedom fizzing like champagne,

Playfully lighting poignant fires

Poem for Linda's Birthday 2022

Look out with a clear mind of yesteryear

Dreaming of those wonderful sublime days

When young, carefree and with nothing to fear

So, relax with a glass of wine and stargaze

Birthdays come only once every year,

Live that fantasy to the extreme

Enjoy the moment without a tear,

Like a satisfied cat that's had its cream

Poem for Megan's Birthday 2022

I'm on the top of my game

Enjoying my salad days

While keeping alive the flame

Seeking knowledge to amaze

Yet, on my birthday relax a little

Celebrate, savour delights, perhaps wine,

And leisurely take my time, life's fickle,

For in the end the day will be sublime

Poem for Lara's Birthday 2022

Longing for long summer days

Away from Uni with friends,

Enjoying new found pleasures,

And special hidden treasures,

That past happiness transcends.

Imagining new found ways

Taking in the summer blaze

Seen through a fine crystal lens

Poem for Roger's Birthday 2022

King Roger visits his wide realm

Sampling fine things that it provides,

Always with his hand on the helm,

Enjoying the pleasant waysides

Admiring cars and doughnut shops,

His lovely garden veg and fruit,

Throughout careful inspection ops,

At times giving his car a toot

Ukraine's Fate

The war in Ukraine rages on,

More atrocities uncovered.

Utter madness and denial

Will there be a war crimes trial?

Russian people their eyes shuttered

Fed on phoney information

From Kremlin demonization,

Brainwashed, everyday lives dark shadowed

Ukrainians fight the darkening storm

Amongst intense growing misery,

Waiting for attack on the Donbas

Dug in, waiting for what will come to pass,

Hated Russians fierce delivery

To light the sky with a missile swarm,

A deeply horrendous growing norm,

Hoping for a Pyrrhic victory

Starlike Celandine

Feel damp lush grasses underfoot,

A tingling sensation in loins,

Breaking gemlike gossamer threads,

As arcing fine bright droplets spreads,

Not listening to what other enjoins.

Enjoying where next step is put,

Like Gulliver in Lilliput,

Seeking golden coins

Through trees, leaves from fat buds springing,

Shuffling through yellow celandine,

Dappled light illuminating

Bright petals with star like gilding

In spotted peaceful bowers shine.

They're a spring sensation gleaming

Found in many woodlands dazzling

Ultra-happiness on cloud nine

Changing Times

The village is awakening once more

For updated news about Ukraine war,

Startling atrocious scenes

Seen on their TV screens

But war is far away from their houses

And they're comfortable with their spouses,

With children at play,

Content for the day

Their only struggle, cost of living rise,

For distant war only briefly agonise,

Covid still with them

But the fears now stem

Narcissi flowering golds and paper whites

One of spring's glorious and superb sights,

Give love and pleasure

In ways all treasure

Taking adult minds off depressing times

Rising prices, climate and Putin's crimes,

But kids still have fun

For life just begun

Hidden away in protective bubbles

In a fast-changing world full of troubles

Their future not known

But clues will be shown

Village life goes on with help when needed,

Hold on to old ways, won't be defeated,

Enjoy spring weather,

Happy together

Thelma's Recovery from Knee Operation

Sitting, thoughtful, knee packed with ice,

Relaxing through the day

Knowing my walking will be better

And I will be a new trend setter

Sanguine as a bright ray;

Thinking of Edelweiss

In a Swiss paradise

With those meadows in lustrous array

Days have passed by and I'm walking,

Not very far as yet,

But contented with dreams from my youth,

So much enjoyment, - for in truth

Without phones, or internet,

Life was sweetly simple.

With body so nimble,

Some situations, half regret

Soon will be back to normality

With my friends and others,

Playing Bridge, having pleasant outings,

Having great interest in many things,

Loving garden flowers,

Whiling away the time

Knowing it's not a crime,

Cherishing all of nature's wonders

Languorous Afternoons

Remembering, those languorous afternoons,

Hot sand between my toes,

Sea stretching blue beyond the dunes,

Dreaming - as time slows

Warm from soft sand, hot to the touch,

Bodies baked in the sun,

Golden brown, - tanned and tingled such,

Caressing as tales spun

Stories from Greek mythology,

Nymphs, satyrs and the gods,

When exploring topology

Defying all the odds

So much sensuality sought

In youthful enterprise

That in time sweeter pleasure brought

Seen in your sparkling eyes

To up and away to chase waves

Running across the strand

Knowing that in evening be slaves

To desires fairly fanned

Swimming in the temperate sea,

Loving, laughing, happy

Joyous for the day, body's free,

Knowing I treasure thee

Allergy Attacks

The enemy out there, - Invisible,

Slow drifting from trees, - in air,

Breathing in,

The effects make you - miserable,

Runny eyes, blocked nose, isn't fair,

Aches begin

Atrocious pollen bombs of April and May,

Bad for allergy sufferers,

Knocks you out,

Feeling isolated throughout the day

Indoors away from tree fevers,

Layabout

When the attack is over your head clears,

Cheerfully you feel free once more,

Euphoric,

Ready to take on the world, - no fears,

Even ignored gardens explore,

Plethoric

Day Dream

Quiet, red roofed place

Away from the turmoil of modern day,

A restful space

In the countryside that is far from grey

Course limestone walls,

Golden at dawn and sunset glamourise

Where pleasure sprawls

And poets in ways often eulogise

A flowing stream

Winds slowly towards the distant river

Where waters gleam,

And look on at times with a faint shiver

Remembering storms,

But now quiet with sheep in the meadow,

Where summer warms

The growing lush grasses in time to mow.

Huddled houses

Spread randomly along the village streets.

Few carouses,

Heard on Friday nights when calmness retreats

Soon quiet again,

Even revellers lower their voices,

Down Little Lane,

Where you'd be lucky to see their faces

Time slows, dreams come,

As daylight fades, - merging what you see,

Phantoms become,

Wraiths, faint images in hyperbole

Laissez Faire

Cost of living up, former life denied,

Overrides worries about climate change,

Don't care about long term, up to others.

It's my life now, - sisters and brothers.

No point being in reproachful rage

If humanity's committing suicide

And the whole world is in a mess beside.

For politicians it's tough to assuage

The Mountain

The rough rocky path upwards winds,

Treacherous in places, loose scree,

And precipitous to depths below,

Where in corrie's there's still iced snow.

An environment to feel free,

With challenges of different kinds

For those with ingenious minds

And venturous if under twenty

Finger holds grasping a rock face,

Pulling, pushing, climbing, slowly

Finding a route, - mesmerised.

Seeing a small lily surprised,

Tucked into a pocket, lonely.

Carried on at a faster pace

Until reaching a special place

Where a route went on narrowly

Scrambling upwards to the top,

Seeing more of the mountain chain

That stretched eastward and to the west,

Distant blue grey peaks coalesced

In misty haze to coastal plain.

Sat, looked over a giddy drop,

Warmed by smooth rocks, for a brief stop

- Before moving on again

Setting sun painted the sky red

Illuminating, rosy light,

Ethereal, fleeting feeling

In the gathering mist, haunting.

The way down the ridge a delight,

Down in the valley white cloud spread

And above where purple streaks thread

Felt the joy of scrambling excite

Down the mountain at eventide

Faster now exhilarating

Shadows from jutting rock lengthen,

Some sheer drops with growing tension

In gathering gloom liberating,

Sounds, boots on scree amplified.

Now glad to be down bleary-eyed

Whole experience scintillating

Looked back at the mountain with pleasure

Against a darkening sky, now black

Magnificent, - none the less,

A tough climb - a great success.

On grassy slopes glad to be back,

But such realities treasure

That will be recalled forever.

Continued homewards on the track

Spirits Fanned

Head west for the Welch Marches

To a place near Shobdon Arches.

Those are the wooded borderlands

Where your surreal vision expands

Within historic rolling hills

To experience dream like thrills

- In that land that time forgot

Being rapt in this stunning spot

Wild flower meadows luxurious

And darkened woods mysterious,

Old trails to hidden ancient gems

Revealed in many fine poems

This is a part of old England

Where quietly, life's spirits are fanned,

To settle in the countryside

Immersive in nature, clear-eyed

Jubilee

Celebration of the Queen's jubilee,

Village people so happy and carefree,

Fluttering flags with bunting and street parties

Brings back from the past many memories

Seventy years she has reigned gloriously

With a smile and devotion, wonderfully.

A monarch who's seen us from post war blues

Through changes to no world-wide ballyhoos

Forgotten Empire, sinking Commonwealth,

Less comfortable for our Kingdom's health,

Our future to England and St George

With an identity that we will forge

What future for royalty, who knows,

Could be a new republic, I suppose,

The Queen has seen us through our decline and fall

And now a chance to thank her one and all

Pessimism

Feeling low with a heavy heart,

Dull grey cloud cover overhead,

Depressing days being morose

Feeling the benefit, the most.

In heavy times the depths of dread

When new ideas are torn apart

For citizens are far from smart

Not mindful of blackness ahead

Tretower Castle and Court

Castle ruins stand forlornly

Within a field of sheep feces.

Ruined tower amongst fallen walls

Many years since its noisy halls

And Picard's grip on the Marches.

Nearby an old court stands stinly,

Medieval ruin, moody,

Now in hands of Cadw trustees

Restored slowly from a Welch farm

To approach its former glory

In heyday of the family Vaughan,

Although, still ensuring timeworn

Beneath hills so high and hoary.

Yet, the place has a certain charm

Where there is no fear of harm,

Living with an entwined story

Berrington Hall

In a green wooded pastoral landscape

On a hill spied splendid Berrington Hall

A fine Neo-Palladian mansion

Built in late eighteenth century fashion

That Henry Holland's design did enthrall

And Capability Brown's held agape.

And three families who lived there helped to shape

Until death duties were the downfall

Thomas Harley created the estate

From money made through Government contracts,

But with no male heir through Anne to Rodney's.

Ninety-five years later to the Cawley's,

After Rodney sold all the artefacts,

In the late Fifties National Trust its fate

Assets from elsewhere served to mitigate

Such as from Snowshill Manor old couture

That of late has been topped by a good buy,

A mantua, once owned by Anne Harley.

The dress is displayed in all its glory,

An eighteenth-century gown gem to revivify.

There's also another exhibit with allure

One of the best statuettes seen for sure

In fine rose marble don't pass it by

Round of Upper and Lower Harlestone

Set out from the golf club at Harlestone

Under white cloud dotted sapphire sky

To St Andrew's church that stands alone

It's twelve century tower not so high

Left the war memorial in the grounds,

Marked by its Celtic Cross, to a lane

Shaded by tall trees, hearing no sounds,

Roofs of the village below so plain

Continued uphill beside green woods

Emerging to new lands of rounded hills

In the upper village neighbourhoods

That the old English tranquil scene upfills

Wild flower meadows, childhoods memories,

Goat's Beard and Moon Daisies part of thrills

Set against rooftop homologies

Thatched houses with artistic straw frills

Down in the valley found a rippling stream

Close by a cottage with eyebrows stands,

Comfortable, its rusted stone agleam

In these ancient conserved rural lands

On through floral meadows with stately oaks

And over a golfing fairway to recall

The old house that history invokes,

Pulled down in 1940's, Harlestone Hall

Some say it inspired Mansfield Park

A famous novel by Jane Austen,

But there is no proof, so kept in the dark,

And walked into the clubhouse again

For Thelma's 90th Birthday

There's still a young girl within

With desires and ambitions

But restrained, partly shut in,

With body's aged conditions

What times I've had through changes,

Technology and reforms,

Much sadness and joy phases

With a loving kiss that warms

Savour such golden treasures

Recall many happy days.

Don't go lightly to future shores

Ensure life is kept ablaze

Walks in Old Age

Face to the wind

Blowing cool from the east,

The old man grinned,

His aged face lined and creased

He looked ahead

Thinking, enough today,

Weary way tread,

Tomorrow, come what may

Goals reduced now,

Limbs just not what they were,

Lack strength somehow,

Trying not to despair

Must not give up,

Look forward to summer,

Not as a tup

Out to grass, just bummer

But happy strolls,

Feeling good to walk miles,

Sing barcaroles,

And even enjoy stiles

Wishful Thinking

Again, comes intense heat

With lethargic feelings

Shuttered house, bittersweet,

Naked, winter cravings

Temperature at new highs

No longer live outside,

A climate change prize,

From the blazing sun hide

Oh, to be in England

Of my young salad days

When nature had kind hand,

My lovely childhood phase.

Snapshot of the Donbas

Drifting aimlessly through bombed out streets, stressed,

Blooded brow, staring eyes, a worn-out ghost,

In stained torn vest and tattered trousers dressed

Quiet now after missile attacks suppressed,

All in this dystopian world morose

Thoughts of the nation's former times repressed

Dead bodies lie, the undead dispossessed,

Darkened skies the apocalypse is close,

No longer help expected from the West

Living, shelter from extreme excesses,

Waiting, - waiting for what, as time slows

And destruction of the world progresses

Life's Conveyer

Stand on life's conveyer

Feeling, seeing and smelling

Being a bold stayer

At times quite impelling

Gaining knowledge and facts

From external sources,

Making many contacts,

Joining many courses

In time loosen up more

And journey more widely,

Other things to explore,

Guarding memories tightly

As the pace decreases

And stresses are reduced,

Aware of caprices,

Enjoying, freedom loosed

Soon let down by body,

Conscious of aches and pains,

But never was shoddy,

Yet adapt to these strains

Mind is still bright and clear

With many things to do,

Every day while your here,

Use time it counts for you

Conveyor moves faster,

The end approaches now,

While body is master

What does the mind allow?

For Cicely's Birthday 2022

Time flows on, what's another year?

I'm so young at heart,

I'm a young woman, in my mind,

Although many years left behind,

Dreams come a la carte,

Such memories, no need for a tear,

I've had a good life, it's clear.

Days count, play it smart

Love my family in many ways,

Love my garden and holidays

Love those insights that amaze

Tory Leadership

Do we get another liar

After the demise of Boris,

As the Conservatives conspire

The economy needs a blitz

The Truss without a T, says it all,

He belief in ill considered finance

Would be a disaster, her thoughts banal,

Few will survive her biased game of chance

Rishi is honest about what we face,

But doesn't appeal to grass root Tories

They fear his boldness, background and race

And rather believe in Fairy Stories

UK wants the promises of Brexit,

Although basically based on lies,

With the manifesto will always sex it,

Electorate should look to the future, be wise

Euro Final

Tension builds in the Euro final,

As the game goes into extra time

Fear the match might slip away like vinyl,

A typical German England paradigm

But solved by artful Chloe Kelly

Who scored the difficult winning goal

Through the German underbelly,

The roar of the crowd was England's soul

Chloe stripped off her shirt to wave around

Widely running to be hugged and raised up

Joyfully celebrating to Wembley sound

A loud uproar for they had won the cup

Bad Fall but Lucky

Fell flat on dark black tarmac,

Hitting my nose, head and lips

With a terrible whack,

I thought I'd had my chips

Blood streamed from my sore nose,

As I was on all fours.

Saw four shoes, as I rose,

Head with muzzy uproars

Two men came to assist

Bringing paper towelling,

Out of a conscious mist

Began bloody wiping

Then two black Labradors,

With them a tallish man

Saw I was in the wars,

'Walk with me if you can'

He was a kind doctor,

Asked several questions

Briefly checked me over

After some reflections

Took me to his driveway

Then took me by car home,

Told me, must have a survey

At A & E, don't roam

Spent the next nine hours there

CT scan and X-Ray,

Seven stitches to bear,

With heart tests come what may

In the end sent me home,

Told I was lucky,

Knowing I couldn't roam,

Bad left leg, still plucky

Cicely drove me back,

After a very long day,

For cup of tea and snack

- Happy all the way

Moments

Need to go out and see,

Experience new things,

'Life is not measured by breaths you take,

But moments that take your breath away'

Natural and man-made landscape,

Stimulate imagination,

Life is not measured by breaths you take,

But moments that take your breath away

Explore, be innovative

In shades of science to art

Life is not measured by breaths you take,

But moments that take your breath away

Love until the limits

Wallow in emotions,

Life is not measured by the breaths you take,

But moments that take your breath away

Chapter 2: Essays on Travel & Walks

" One's destination is never a place, but a new way of seeing things."

Henry Miller

"Once you have travelled, the voyage never ends, but is played out over and over again in the quietest chambers. The mind can never break off from the journey."

Pat Conroy

The essays included here are snippets from travels taken in the past and recorded in diaries. They hopefully provide a snapshot of the time and place as I saw it and the discoveries made.

Events in Sighişoara

Sighişoara is an attractive town in the centre of Transylvania in Romania. Long ago it was a Dacian settlement and in the third century BCE was known as Sandova. Later in the second century AD, it became an Imperial Roman Castrum and was used as a base for fighting legions. No evidence of these ancient settlements remains today.

Probably an early German community was established as a village that had a fortified refuge located on the Castle Hill, but this was destroyed by a Tatar invasion of 1241. Shortly afterwards it was rebuilt and the Dominicans in 1289 took interest in it as a place for a monastery. Later, in the 14th century, German colonists, mainly craftsmen, settled there. The town was eventually fortified with curtain walls and towers that surrounding the hill, as a protection against Ottoman invasions, for these were a continual threat. By the 15th century these defenses were reinforced with walls 15m high with 14 defensive towers, though today only nine of these original towers remain. During the town's expansion it played both an important strategic, as well as a commercial role, and became one of the most important towns of Transylvania. German artisans and craftsmen dominated the urban economy. It is a fact that the first mention of Sighişoara as the town's name was in the fifteenth century at the time of Vlad Dracul of Wallachia. Coins were minted in the town and his son Vlad Tepes born there in 1431.

During travels in Romania in 2011 with my wife Cicely and friends Roger and Linda approached Sighişoara on a glorious day from the west where we had been visiting the 'Saxon Villages'. Drove along the Strada Corneşti. It was an impressive view with the old town, dominating the surroundings, high on a hill to our right. Followed the contours of the hill along Strada Morii and parked opposite the Tourist Information Centre located in Piaţa Octavian Goga. There found that a young woman in the Tourist Office who spoke good English. I asked her whether we could drive up to the old town. She told us if we were to drive on further around the hill, we would find a road going up to it. I left with a town map full of confidence.

Roger drove off impatient to find the way up. Reaching Piaţa Hermann Oberth found it was a hive of activity. People were strolling in the sunshine around a little park like area, or sitting in one of the many cafés. Roger spotted by the side of the park a narrow road that led up the hill and took in his head to drive up.

Stradeta Turnului is a steep narrow lane. After about 150m, before the clock tower, came across barriers placed across the road. Finding that he could not drive up into the old town and also was difficult to turn around turned left around a tight hairpin bend to go down the even narrower Stradeta Cetăţii in hope that it would take us back down to the square again. Unfortunately for us a small lorry plus a trailer that was collecting rubbish from bins turned the corner from the square and drove up towards us. Two of the men who were collecting bins at the roadside waved for us to back up, but Roger was having none of it. He switched off the engine and got out of the car. He said to them in loud English waving his hand and pointing to his eyes, "I can't back up, I'm blind".

There was a standoff. At first the lorry driver looked like he was going to back up but gesticulations and expletives from the bin collection men stopped him. Roger seemed rather angry and put out so I got out of the car to help as Roger got back in. He started reversing fast back up the hill with me guiding him for it was very difficult with the narrowness and with steps jutting out from roadside houses, as well as the hazard of bins in the street. He slipped the clutch and the acceleration caused it to burn resulting in much smoke and smell, fumes became overpowering. Eventually he reached the top in a cloud of gases and smoke and eased over to one side. When the bin lorry arrived, the men insisted he back up off the road because the lorry couldn't get by. Fortunately, there was a gateway to one of the houses where he could do so. When they eventually passed us and drove on there was no thanks given, though Roger seemed relieved, even though the clutch still smelled awful.

Reached the square again without any further trouble and drove on around the citadel rock to find a way up. Above us noticed an area with a large number of trees that we soon discovered was a cemetery. A tree shaded road, Strada Ilarie Chendi, cut up hill at the side of the cemetery wall, so we followed it. Then proceeded around to Strada Anton Pann to find at last a road that ramped up hill to our right. It had a ticket barrier and paid 15 lei to enter. A pavé road took us on upwards to a 15th century gateway with two arches, named Turnal

Croitorilor. Passed on through it and drove on to a pedestrianized square, the Piața Cetății. In a smaller square, adjacent to it and defined by flowering plants in large planters, a few people sat outside of cafés. Roger though, turned right along the Strada Scolii to park in a space outside a hotel.

Walked across the pavé in sunshine to a vacant table outside the pensuinea café in the shade as the day was already warm. Drinks came quickly. I sipped my iced-coffee while watching two young women carrying large bunches of flowers. Cicely said she had seen on TV that it was the first day back to school and traditionally the children at some schools gave flowers to their teachers, quite a lovely idea that might improve things in the UK.

Having relaxed a little set off to explore the town the girls sticking together and Roger and I splitting up. First of all, I went down to the Clock tower off the Piața Muzeului passing by Casa Vlad Dracul and Casa Venețiană both fine old three-storey houses. The Clock Tower, Turnul cu Ceas, is an important feature in the town. In fact, it is the most impressive and picturesque of the nine remaining towers. Its original role was the main gateway into the citadel and was also used to accommodate the town's council. Built in the second half of the 14th century it was modified and in the 16th century raised in height to 64m. After a fire in 1676, caused by an explosion in the town's gunpowder store, the roof of the tower was restored to the current ornate Baroque shape. This was further embellished in 1894 by use of coloured tiles. The four small corner turrets indicate that the town had judicial autonomy with the 'right of sword'. This was the right to convict criminals to death. In the 17th century a clock was installed with a wooden horologe and in 1648 was remodeled by Johann Kirschel. He equipped the clock with two large dials, one for each façade of the tower gateway and with two groups of wooden figurines arranged in niches. Importantly, the figurines are activated by the clock's mechanism. On the clock's citadel side, the Goddess of Peace holds an olive branch and by her side a drummer beats the hours on his bronze drum. Above them there are the Goddess of Fairness holding a balance and the Goddess of Justice with a spade accompanied by two angels representing day and night. At 6 am the angel symbolizing the day comes out, marking the beginning of the working day and at 6 pm the angel symbolizing the night comes out, carrying two burning candles in his hands and marks the end of the working day and the arrival of evening. I looked closely yet saw no movement of the figures, or at any other time I passed by whilst in Sighişoara.

I went back up to the street to where we had left the car and had a look at the top end of it where the Scara Acoperitã ascended to the Church-on-the-Hill. This is a gothic building that that replaced the original fortress during building operations between 1345 and 1525. The staircase is next to School Street and fascinatingly is a covered wooden stairway named appropriately the 'Covered Stairs', or 'Schoolboys' Stairs' in English translations. It was built in 1642 to assist children on their way up to the School on the Hill, as well as churchgoers' during inclement weather. Originally the stairs had 300 steps, but today their number has been reduced to 175. I didn't go up the steps, but Roger told me later that he did, instead I walked back to the clock tower and passed through the arched gateway to descend to the lower town, looking as I went through the gate at the reverse side of the clock.

On the lower town side of the clock there is a second niche holding a figurine, which is said to represent an executioner, as well a second drummer. Above them there are seven figurines representing pagan gods who represent the days of the week, Diana, Mars, Mercury, Jupiter, Venus, Saturn and the Sun. These figurines sit on a rotating disk that turns at midnight marking a change of day. The clock mechanisms are still supposed to work. Restoration during 1906 was improved in 1964 by an electric motor drive.

Disappointed that I saw no movement of the figures I carried on down the narrow pavé surfaced lane passing by a loggia, a covered walkway, possibly for use in winter time. It is constructed with wooden beams and with a tiled sloping roof, all set against a stone wall. Both the lane and the loggia walkway led down to an old house built across the passage with tunnel archway under it for access. Walking on through it reached the road that Roger had driven up earlier before his 'clutch-burning-spree' and carried on down it to emerge into Piaţa Hermann Oberth.

People were taking lunch at tables outside of brightly decorated restaurants colourfully enhanced with pots of red pelargoniums standing outside. Other people were gathered in the small park area having picnic al fresco lunches. The sky so clear and intensely blue. The air temperature was probably already in the upper twenties.

I walked over to the main road keeping to the shade as much as possible and made my way down Strada Decembrie 1918 to find a money exchange. The rate was excellent at 4.9 lei to the GB Pound. After exchanging some money walked through into Piata Octavian Goga to walk a little way up Strada Morii where I stood for a while in the shade by a shop doorway.

I looked carefully at the town map I had picked up at the tourist office. Then looked across to Castle Hill and Turnul Cositorarilor that stuck out above leafy trees, both bathed in sunlight. In English it is called the Tinker's Tower and canon ball damage was still visible in the walls. Up the hill saw the slit windows of the fusiliers' gallery, the Turnul Tăbăcarilor, or Tanners' Tower in English, further around the walls. This is one of the oldest towers and was built to protect the main gate's interior court.

I felt a gentle tap on my shoulder and turned to see Linda and not too far behind, Cicely. They had been trying to find Roger for they couldn't contact him on his mobile. They said that they had been to a spoon-maker working in the street that led down to the Clock Tower from the old town's main square. Cicely wanted to buy some spoons and needed some currency. I gave her a few hundred Lei and told her that I was going further up the street to some steps to see other monuments, they said they would follow for a while.

The steps were just a short way up the road towards the

square where the tourist office is situated that we visited earlier. They rose sharply at first to ascend the hill, but soon turned sharply left almost parallel to the contours yet still below the old town walls. Eventually a stair alley led to the base of Turnal Fierarilor, the Blacksmith's Tower. It was built in 1631 in place of the Old Barber's Tower and is constructed on a rectangular plan. It appears quite tall and large from the outside, but inside the walls are lower compared to others. I turned right to follow a path below the old town walls, while the girls whom had followed me so far left me and carried on towards the Clock Tower to buy their spoons.

I carried on around the walls looking for an opening in them. Below me, through trees, saw a patchwork of reddish-brown town roofs and had glimpses of the River Tărnava Mare way beyond.

Eventually walked in an anticlockwise direction to the northeast side of the hill where I came across an opening in the walls to enter the shady grounds of Sf. Iosi, a Roman Catholic Church. It was built in 1894 on a demolition site of an earlier Franciscan monastery. To the right of the church is a small park and down from it the Turnal Cizmarilor, The Shoemakers Tower. This tower has had several reconstructions the latest being in 1681 when it was rebuilt under the architectural influence of the Baroque period. Originally the front of the tower was an artillery bastion, but this was demolished in 1846. The tower has a pointed spire shaped roof and a covered outside staircase leads up to a second floor.

Crossed over the park to one of the old town's narrow

roads to walk down Strada Tămplarilor towards the centre of the old town. On the way passed by a colourful mixture of single and two-storey town houses, their walls washed in various pastel shades of green, pink and yellows. Reaching Strada Zidul Cetății saw to my right the town's large 14th century gateway, Turnal Croitorarilor, known as the Tailors' Tower, which we had driven in through earlier. I didn't go for a closer look but turned left to the Piața Cetății. There I met Roger in the square, he had been up on the hill through the covered staircase and guessed that I had gone down into the lower town to get some money. The girls were still buying spoons, so I went down to them to see how they were getting on.

Mark Tudose is a wood carver extraordinaire he claims. He likes to tell a story and his wooden spoons have many stories to tell. His great idea is to make an apparently simple object valuable through its story illustrated by symbols. In life, he says,

"People search consciously or unconsciously, for just a few simple things: love, happiness, luck, wisdom; with my spoons, I am telling Romanian folk tales which deal with these spiritual elements. Among my spoons you will find the spoon of luck, the spoon of lovers, the spoon of the good and evil and so on."

Asking him why spoons? He says,

"I wanted to work with spoons because it's a craft 100% Romanian and because there are so many designs to serve me as inspiration. For example, did you know that Romania has the largest collection of wooden spoons in

the world? You can see over 5,300 models at the Wooden Spoons Museum (Muzeul Lingurilor de lemn - Ion Tugui) in Campulung Moldovenesc. It's a fascinating thing to see, really."

Mark learnt this traditional Romanian trade from his grandfather and Mark's family are all wood carvers, including his mother and his sisters. Throughout the year, he travels with his spoons to craft fairs all around the country. The girls were lucky to find him on the streets of Sighişoara, his adoptive city he likes so much. He first visited Sighişoara in 2005 and says.

"It was love at first sight,"

So, he decided to leave behind the capital city of Bucharest to live in the place of his dreams.

Cicely bought the 'Power Spoon' and the 'Luck Spoon' and his story behind these is as follows.

The snake is a symbol of power, but at the same time is known as the protector spirit of the house, or "the one who defends the citadel's gates" Also the flag of the Dacian people used to be represented by a serpant (or dragon). Its head was made of iron, and the rest made of leather. This way, when the wind blew into the dragon's mouth, it would sound like a wolf howling, which would discourage the enemy and scare any horses that weren't used to the sound.

The stork is a symbol of luck. In Romanian folk tradition they used to say that when a stork makes her nest on a house she protects it from fire, water and thieves.

When all transactions and goodbyes were finished, I asked the girls to follow me up School Street to a shop. It was on the left-hand-side higher up, situated near to the covered stair. I wanted to show them some traditional garments as well as a shop selling all types of things. It was in this latter shop that Cicely bought a doll for our great niece Emilia. After they had explored the shops and some of the attractive yards at the back of them walked back to the car to find Roger standing by the side of it. He had been looking at a menu displayed on the outside of Hotel Sighişoara, an attractive place decked out with baskets of red pelargoniums. He had also had a look around it and suggested we had a snack lunch there. It seemed a great idea to us all, so went in.

Discovered it dated back to the 16th century. It looked attractive and out back was a large patio area with pergolas covered in ivy that shaded wooden tables set with crisp white linen tablecloths. Sat at one pondering on the contents of the menu while we ordered drinks. At first there seemed to be no agreement on what we should have to eat for we couldn't just get one plate of mixed things, the waiter said it wasn't possible, so three of us decided on a plate of 'Caprese' to share. Roger though ever the bon viveur opted out, he wanted a main vegetarian course with frites. Thinking that one Caprese wouldn't be enough we ordered two. However, when our orders arrived each plate of Caprese had 4 Bruschettas plus lines of thick slices of beefy tomatoes alternating in stack form with thick slabs of cheese, the two plates quite ambitious for a snack lunch for three of us. But thinking our plates were a challenge I only had to look at Roger's enormous selection and quantity on an extremely large platter it made our offering shrink into gastronomic insignificance. His plate had Macedonian salad, aubergine fritters, courgette fritters, boiled potatoes, cauliflower, broccoli and slices of cucumber and tomato. In the end Linda, Cicely and I finished one and a half plates of Caprese, but Roger's plate had hardly been attacked even though Linda was asked to help him out little. Unfortunately, it remained a mass of uneaten food.

Throughout the meal heard parts of a conversation from an adjacent table where a large extended Romanian family sat. Some judging by their accents had come from America. It was a celebratory meal of some sort where different dishes were passed to children and adults alike.

Later left Sighişoara heading eastwards, it had been a good visit but could have done with more time, possibly a night and another half day to see all the sites. It is indeed magnificent old town and was obviously well cared for by its citizens.

School Teachers with Flowers

Town Clock

Sighişoara from the Lower Town

Mark Tudose Wood Carver Extraordinaire

Landscape and Rock Phallus's of Cappadocia

Çavusin, is one of the oldest settlements in Cappadocia situated in central turkey and only a mile from Göreme where we were staying in a cave hotel. One day decided to drive on up into the modern village to have a brief look from a distance at a large rock face where troglodyte dwellings used to be until rock falls of 1996 occurred, during an earthquake. This catastrophe drove the remnant population out. Since then, the village has been almost deserted. During our short visit saw only one horse drawn cart.

Exploring this fascinating landscape further it became more open with columnar structures that rose up out of the earth amongst low hills called colloquially, 'fairy chimney's. These chimneys increased in number at a place called Pasabaglan, 'Monks Valley', where we stopped at a collection of market stalls at the side of the road to explore. The chimneys here had multiple heads and substantial conical bases. In places the worn fine tuff mounded in hills like sand hills. A few scrubby trees gave shade to stalls and in other places ropes hung between branches of trees over which carpets were hung. Strolled for a while under an intense blue sky amongst the tall columns admiring the colouration changes from tuff to basalt. In one spot a camel lay where it was tethered to a large stone. Noticed many of the columns had caves within them.

Millions of years ago volcanic ash rained down of the landscape. In time the ash hardened off into tuff, a porous rock covered by a layer of basalt. Over the following centuries a process of erosion began. Through the millennia the soft tuff wore down forming residual pillars that stand as tall as 40m. The harder basalt eroded much more slowly such that the pillars have a conical like cap.

'Fairy Chimneys' are remarkable. They look like erect phalluses, some of which are multi-stemmed. Walking in amongst them found further market stalls erected between them. Some of the rock stems had caves within them, these had been cut out of the soft rock. They were probably used in the past by hermits, or for chapels. One fairy chimney hermit abode had three heads and at its base an entrance tunnel carved out of the white tuff rock. There was also in one a chapel dedicated to St Simeon.

St Simeon was a strange character who lived in the fifth century near to Aleppo. Allegedly he became disturbed by rumours that he worked miracles and took to living on top of a two-metre-high column. He later moved to a higher one of fifteen metres, only climbing down for food and drink left for him by his disciples. All hermits of Cappadocia though didn't resort to living on top of columns, but rather in hollowed out local tuff columns with rooms at the top. They got food and drink from kind locals via buckets raised and lowered by rope. Social security in those days was cheap.

Later a journey from Kaymakli took us into new territory heading eastward through an agrarian countryside under a blazing sun. Saw many types of crops grown in large rolling fields spread out before us across an undulating landscape. In one place, coloured masses of ripened orange pumpkins, rows upon rows of them stretched out to the horizon. Stopped for a brief while at the road side to take a more careful look. A gentle welcome breeze disturbed leaves on a row of poplars situated on top of a nearby hill, twinkling gold in the late afternoon sunshine, amplifying the magic of the place.

Driving on once more saw a number of people working in groups within large open fields that bordered the road. They were gathering in their potato harvest. Sacks being filled with the crop and loaded onto flat-bed trailers that were coupled to tractors. Some tractors that were already on the road towing their large loads eastward, as we continued onwards following them. It looked as if the whole world around us had been called out to harvest the crop. I had never seen so many potatoes before. Soon the road began to descend from the high plain to a wooded valley. At the bottom saw a village spread out along it with many old houses and caves situated in cliffs above. The tractors stopped at a large cave entrance on the outskirts of the village where sacks were being off-loaded and taken into it for storage. The caves would provide an ideal environment for storage, the darkness and a constant temperature, always cooler or warmer than the outside throughout the year.

Drove on down into the valley to enter the village of Sahinefendi where men in black salvar trousers sat on benches chatting at roadside cafés and groups of women, covered from head to toe in colourful garments, dusty from a day's work in the fields, also gathered and talked together. Inquisitively, all eyes turned to watch us, as we drove through their settlement.

Drove on through following the river, a tributary to the Kizihrmak, or the Red River, northwards. The Red River is the longest in Turkey. There were no fairy chimneys to be seen but saw outstanding rock features on the far side of the wooded valley. Surreal red rock mesas reflected the last rays from the sun, their cliff like slopes in partial shadow highlighting a convoluted topology. On through the village of Takinpasa and on to Cemil the sky already darkening after sunset. Stopped at the roadside to look up a narrow road leading up to a gorge where part of an old village was located piled high against a cliff on top of which were further houses and what looked to be a bell tower.

Further up the valley passed through Mustafapasa and on to the picturesque town of Ürgüp. The road took us up through it passing by some large fine old houses. These probably, according to the 'Rough Guide' were once Greek owned prior to the exchange of populations between Greece and Turkey in 1923, before then the town had a largely Greek population. Within the town a large conspicuous citadel rock had numerous caves cut within it. Many people were about in the streets and it looked like a thriving community

The road climbed westward and after a short while stopped just off road where other people had gathered to watch the sunset. There was still enough light, at the elevated location. Close by below the ridge and white tuff dunes were 'fairy chimneys'. Looked down to a valley that ran toward Göreme, Zelve and the plain beyond, on towards far off Avanos. Pinkish-purple tinges lit up distant hills and mesas and illuminated the warm rust-brown patches and topknots of the 'fairy chimneys'. The structures added a romantic feeling in the fading light. Drove on once more to Göreme and to our fine cave rooms in the Kelebek Hotel.

A few days later on our way back towards Göreme after further daily excursions in the countryside asked Roger to stop the car and let us out. Cicely and I wanted to visit 'Love Valley' before leaving the area the following day. He dropped us off near to a footpath we thought was the right one to take, unfortunately it wasn't. Roger drove up and down the road a few times trying to locate the right one before dropping us off near to a new large new hotel.

The footpath wanted wasn't easy to find, so walked back downhill towards the village looking over high grassy banks at the edge of the road, but only found small cultivated lots and ruinous houses. Puzzled walked back to the new hotel and at a gatehouse asked the way from the guard on duty. He couldn't help much, but pointed down the road back towards the Open-air Museum where at the bottom of the hill a market stall stood at the entrance to a footpath. It looked a definite possibility so walked down towards it and found to our relief a sign indicating to 'Zemi Valley'.

Following the footpath for a short way came to a fork in it and took the right-hand track. Stopped to look at what appeared to be an extended family harvesting pumpkin in a dusty field now devoid of greenness. A toddler was trying with all his might to toss pumpkins into a trailer almost full. Nearby, women bent to cut more. They were colourful in their long flowery skirts with long unmatched flowery long-sleeved tops. Scarves covering their heads added to the whole pleasurable effect. The men were dressed in Western Style with open necked shirts and jeans. They were helping to load pumpkins on to a trailer attached to a tractor.

Walking on followed a fence around to a sandy path that took us up over a bank of white tuff with patches of course ripened grasses to join another track for a short way before turning right to take a dusty trail up a steep rise towards large conical rock structures on 'Sunset Hill'. The path climbed upwards to the right passing by large columns of rock and between them looked down into a valley in which tall erect stone penises reached for the sky: this had to be 'Love Valley'.

Tarried a while within this enchanting place not quite understanding how the columns were formed, why so many and why not more substantial mesas instead. Further up the path two girls sat looking out at the columns in the fading light of late afternoon silently contemplating the many erect forms.

It was getting late so walked back the way we had come. Near a tall conical rock, which looked at one time had been lived in, was a paddock with some fine horses and lying nearby an Alsatian dog guarded a large litter of puppies.

Walked to Göreme, passing the grounds of the new hotel again with the guardhouse and on uphill to the outskirts of the village. From there it was downhill to the Avanos Road. Turned left there into the village's main street. Passed by now lit restaurants, a carpet shop, tourist offices, a bank and so on through the centre of the village and up to the bus station to walk on up the steep cobbled road back to the cave Kelebek Hotel and 'Flintstone' rooms that were well furnished and comfortable, not like the American animated sitcom.

Pasabaglan, 'Monks Valley'

Pumpkins and Poplars

Pumpkin Harvest near Zemi Valley

Rock Formations 'Love Valley'

Pano Platres and the mountain Villages of the Troodos

It was back in November of 2003 that Cicely and I spent several days in Platres, Cyprus, and explored its environs. We had been staying previously for the night at a Taverna at San Socretes that was a disaster and best forgotten. Previously on arrival in Tochni were told that that the hotel we had booked into was closed for the season and as a result been transferred to a Taverna, and as it was late in the day and dark had to accept this.

The next day checked out and drove off in glorious sunshine making up for the previous evening and night. Before driving on to the Troodos visited the Archaeological site at Choirokoitia. Cicely stayed in the car while I went to look around. A man at the ticket office was the only person seen. There I paid seventy-five cents to enter.

The site has a World Heritage status and is one of the most important prehistoric places in the Eastern Mediterranean. Only part of the area had been excavated but what has been found is a Neolithic settlement occupied from 9000 to 7000 years ago and situated on the slopes of a hill within a loop of the Maroni River. Some reconstruction work had been done to illustrate 9000 -year-old round houses with flat roofs.

I took a track up hill to view three areas of excavations. There was evidence of numerous buildings and a pathway that ran through them. The place much older than remains I had seen on Malta. In a book I purchased further detail was given of the excavations and interpretations of the findings. It seems that the settlers were farmers from the Near East mainland and had a social structure for collective effort to the common good. A house consisted of several circular buildings equipped with hearths and basins and arranged around a small courtyard where domestic activities took place. Interestingly the houses belonged to both the living and the dead, who were buried in pits beneath rammed earthen floors. Various tools have been found made from stone or bone, stone vessels, vegetal and animal remains and anthropomorphic figurines in stone and clay. A complex access to the village has also been uncovered with defensive walls.

Returned to the car and Cicely and drove off along the Limosol road before turning off towards Platres. Climbed steadily through foothills and barren brush and on through vineyards until reaching extensive pinewoods. The climb steep for most of the way with many twists and turns. At last reached Pano Platres at a height of 1082m, a beautiful looking village situated amongst leafy trees.

Apparently, the village has existed since the Lusignan Era of 1192 to 1489. It has a small residential population probably no more than 300, but rises to thousands in high season when tourists make it their base, for it is the largest resort and is situated only 5km from Troodos Square a focus of mountain trails. Many famous people have been resident for a while including King Farouk of

Egypt, Giorgos Seferis and Daphne du Maurier who wrote the majority of her novel Rebecca while in Platres.

It was around midday when I parked the car near the centre and spotted the Petite Palace Hotel where we were to stay but decided to have a drink and a snack at a café-bar first. Sat outside feeling a cold wind blowing. In its heyday Platres was known as a second Simla. Simla being the summer capital of the British Raj in the state of Himachai Pradesh, India. Platres then is regarded as attractive in high summer as a place of refreshing climate.

About two thirty after checking into the hotel changed into our walking gear and set off to Kalidonia Falls. The start was a good fifteen-minute walk up hill out of the village before reaching the start of the trail. A notice board informed us that the trail was only 2km to the falls.

Entered a wooded valley following a stream, called the Cold-Water River. Walked in the shade of trees, mainly pine but black poplars and oaks too. Zigzaged our way crossing and recrossing the stream by stepping stones within the boulder strewn valley. Gnarled tree roots at times were a hazard hidden in the thick vegetation amongst ivy covered trees and shrubs. At times though had more open views of a distant beautiful wooded landscape. Climbing ever upwards it seemed that we would never get to the falls with sounds of water splashing over rocks ever with us. After about three quarters of an hour walking began to think of turning back but instead with confidence pressed on further, determined to see the falls. At last were rewarded at dark pool the full glory above us of tumbling water from a great height splashing into the pool. I learned later the height of the falls is around 12m.

Didn't stay long fearing the sun would set before reaching the end of the trail in Platres. Found it much easier walking downhill and reached the end by a quarter past four, the sun setting around quarter of an hour later.

Back in our hotel room with the radiator full on for warmth. Fortunately, the radiator had been adjusted by the hotel staff while we away as the temperature falls rapidly after dark. Quickly showered and changed and went down to the bar to have a drink and read before our evening meal.

It was around quarter to seven as we went in to dinner finding only one other couple in the restaurant. Ordered the house white wine to accompany the meal which started with a chicken and potato soup, followed by a tomato salad and a moussaka main course. Later had a dessert of a honey and almond filo wrap. It was an excellent meal and satisfied our appetite since the walk. Praised madame for her cooking before retiring to our room.

The next day woke to a glorious morning and looked out from our balcony at the colourful surrounds of autumn with warm glowing shades of reds to yellows. Later at breakfast there was plenty of choice; besides cereals, yoghurt and honey there were plates of meats, cheeses and boiled eggs, as well as dishes of cucumber and beautiful ripe tasty tomatoes. Enjoyed the breakfast and talked to madame about the flood in the room we had

had while showering. She offered us another room without hesitation and Cicely went off to inspect it. While she was away, I talked to madame and found out that they had bought the place in 1996. She told me about things to do in the area and keen on us walking the 'Atlanta Trail' around Mount Olympus and said it was an ideal day to walk it. When Cicely returned said that the other room was noisy and would keep the room we had.

Told Cicely about madame's suggestion for a walk and she agreed that we should do it. First though went over to an attractive shop to buy things for lunch; bought biscuits and some persimmons and also put in our backpacks some of the oranges we had picked up at the taverna in Tochni.

Had a pleasant drive from Platres up the Troodos, the sky a cerulean blue and in the bright morning sunlight the woods reflected a golden light. After a steep climb to the village at the top situated at 1707m parked in Troodos Square where there was a collection of shops and accommodation for skiing and walking groups. The Troodos, meaning mountains of Adonis, are the largest mountain range in Cyprus and located about the centre of the island. The highest peak is called Mount Olympus and rises to 1952m.

Within the environs of the mountains are secluded valleys, mountain villages, and Byzantine churches, as well as monasteries and mines. The mines have been known since antiquity since the name of Cyprus itself derives from the Greek word for copper. Mining for the mineral has taken place since 2500 BCE. The real feeling of a village at Troodos Square probably only occurs at the height of the tourist seasons of high summer and winter skiing for it was quiet with few people around.

Sat in the car in an almost empty neat pavé laid car park and changed into our walking gear. It was around ten before starting out on the well-marked trail. The 14km long trail is named after Atalanta of Greek mythology. Allegedly, she was raised by a she-bear after her father abandoned her because he wanted a son. She later developed into a fierce hunter. When she was reunited with humans, she proved a better hunter than men whom she eschewed and made an oath of virginity to Artemis the goddess of moon and hunting.

Walked on through pine woods in a big loop seeing patches of snow here and there. After about a kilometre the surrounds became more open with fewer trees. Old grey-white gnarled junipers dotted the mountainside and further on looked down and out the coast. Nearer to spied a shimmering lake. Continued on clockwise around the mountain, the trail following a contour seeming almost flat. It was very quiet the silence only broken by an occasional raucous crow and twittering of small birds. Took delight in the variety of trees some in clusters of semi woodland.

About a third of the distance along the trail clouds bubbled up ominously from the south. Although appearing lower down than us headed for one of the valleys we had recently left behind. Stopped for a drink and lunch watching the developing weather.

Continued onwards along the trail for the weather didn't seem to be getting any worse. Several signs appeared along the trail indicating a plant to watch out for, a special tree, or the geology of the rocks, or mine-workings. Saw minerals in a white rock with green bands. A notice informed us of its geology as harzburgite with dunite. Chromite grains also sparkled in the rock. Harzburgite, named for its occurrence in the Harz Mountains of Germany, is a ultramatic igneous rock consisting mostly of olivines and enstatite and also contains a few percent of chromium rich spinels.

Shortly afterwards approached a boarded-up mine. The information pamphlet that we had with us from the start of the trail informed us that the mine was opened in 1950 by the Hadjipavlou Company to mine chrome. Tunnelling ceased operation in 1954, but was started up again in 1974 and continued mining activities for eight years before eventual closure. A total of fifteen thousand tons of highly concentrated mineral was exported in that time. It was not apparent how they got the ore off the mountain and could see no environmental damage around us as clues.

The trees became thicker again as we proceeded around the mountain with glimpses of the north coast through them. Saw fine monastery far below us to the west. It felt colder and the further we went on snow lay on the path and in amongst the trees. Reaching the end of the trail saw part of the radar station built near to the peak of Olympus.

Walked on along a metalled road where we saw a man taking photographs of a large snowball before leaving it to take a forest trail back to Troodos Square. It had taken just over four hours to complete the whole circuit. More people were there with a lot more cars in the car park, stalls bustling with trade.

Drove back to Platres under a clear blue sky our near surroundings bathed that golden light, yet to the south thick cloud remained.

Found a restaurant in the square for coffee and a sandwich. The sandwich appearing at our table as a ham and cheese roll served with chips and a salad. Relaxed for a while discussing the walk and scenery before returning to our warm room and a hot shower. Later wrote in my diary the experiences of the day so far before going down to the lounge for a beer before dinner. As before madame did us proud with her home cooking. For starters had dips and a large Greek-salad, followed by roast lamb and potatoes and a dessert of coconut cake. The local white wine flowed with our conversation throughout the meal.

Woke the next morning, a Saturday, to a spectacular clear sky with the view from our balcony enhanced by the early morning light glittering off golden leaves of the surrounding woodland.

Had a good breakfast before setting off to take the Madari Ridge Walk. Drove up to Troodos Village then took a road down towards Nicosia. The car radio was playing and a programme that was informing about

Haikus. I hadn't heard of this type of Japanese poetry before but became interested and began to compose some in my head as we drove along. Its form is three lines of five syllables, seven syllables and five syllables respectively that tell a story, or create and image.

Saw just after passing through Pano Amandos an ugly scar on the mountainside from asbestos mining and carried on to a cross roads, but drove straight on to Kyperounta, a large sprawling village in the eastern Troodos. Just after entering the village turned left on a good metalled road towards Spilia. Not far from Kyperounta after climbing out of a valley where masses of yellow gilded grape vines littered hillside terraces reached the top of a hill where there was a small car park. This is the start point of the Madari Trail and called, 'Doxa si o theos', meaning 'Praise God'.

A well posted trail took us immediately up a steep hillside through enchanting woodland and scrub with a mixture of pines and cedars and an under-cover of cistus, sorbus, berberis and other small bushes mostly Cyprian endemics with white asphodel in clumps dotted here and there. The pleasant smell of pine in the morning heat heightened our senses. The path skirted the left-hand-side of the hill to reach a large boulder outcrop where there were good stands of pine surrounding it. Through the trees spied the Mesaoria Plain that extends across the island from the Bay of Famagusta in the east to Morphou in the west. The path continued upwards to the summit of the hill slightly on its western side. Below us in the valley looked down on Kyperounta, the panoramic scenery filled us with pleasure and amazing views.

The haiku I composed is,

From Madari Ridge

Peer at Mesaoria Plain

To far Turkish lands

We were now on the ridge where another hill rose before us. First walked down through oak woods. I believe that there are three species to be found in Cyprus, but we spotted only two the deciduous Infectoria, probably the sub species Veneris and the shorter evergreen Coccifera probably the sub species Calliprinos. The former with long acorns and the latter a shorter and squat round type. Some of the taller oaks looked quite old. Along the way found benches at good viewing points carefully positioned in shade. The path continued around the hill and ahead of us spotted three peaks. One with a repeater station and the Fire Departments 'Look-Out', peak Adelfi, which we assumed to be our eventual destination.

Walked downhill at first descending and passing through more oaks to reach a col where young Cyprus Cedars grouped with pines and juniper. Here we had amazing views to our left and right-hand-side. To the left the plain towards the Turkish Zone in soft focus because of filtering by an inversion layer, but saw villages and the northern coastline and to our right Kyperounter and vineyards. Behind us the Troodos and Mount Olympus was darkened by a forested covering.

The path steeply climbed once more making for the final ridge walk. It zig-zagged through trees until breaking cover on the high ridge with tremendous views all around. Only a few junipers were striving to survive with some low scrub. Our destination was clearly defined on a conical peak that looked to be a hut that was situated there.

The track ascended and lead us to an excellent vantage point where we sat a while taking in the awesome inspiring beauty and enormous scale of observation. Ahead of us was the bare rocky conical peak of Adelfi. Walked on skirting the peak on the northern side and down to a small car parking area at the head of a road from the south. A number of people were gathered there, but some had already left for a path that descended the north side. Seeing a way up to the top of the peak climbed it to a picnic area outside of the Lookout Station with tables and benches convenient for us to sit and eat our packed lunch.

Clouds had developed over Mount Olympus in the far distance where we saw the golf ball radar station and other ariels. Vision had cleared over the plain to the north and saw more detail than before of the scattered white villages and particularly of the mountain chain along the Kyrenia Peninsular in the Turkish Zone. It was a magnificent viewing point. To the east mountains receded to the very far distance with shades of lavender to blue grey. And along Madari Ridge looked at the way we had walked in the morning.

Went back the way we had come in still glorious sunshine. Passed clumps of peonies gone to seed and stopped at times to view the exceptional landscape with long afternoon shadows highlighting intricate details of the topology. Getting at last to the final descent took it slowly soaking up the atmosphere of woods and rock, startling boulder outcrops and lonely twisted pines. It had been an enjoyable walk taking four hours when we finally arrived back at the car. Estimated the distance to be 13 km and a climb up to 1612m at Adelfi.

Drove from the warmth of the walk to higher and cooler surroundings under grey cloud of Troodos Square, the temperature indicated five degrees Celcius. Went into a restaurant by the tourist centre for coffee then later drove back to Platres arriving in glorious sunshine at around a quarter past four. After showering and changing at the hotel went to the bar for drinks before dinner. Dinner again just what we wanted after a day's walking. Started with soup followed by a salad, then a main course of pork cooked with coriander and cumin spices accompanied by stuffed tomatoes, courgettes and roast potatoes. The local white wine flowed pleasurably throughout the meal. Finally, a dish of local grapes was brought to us with our coffee.

The next day, a Sunday, woke once more to sunshine with not a cloud in the sky, another delightful morning. After a good breakfast set out for Cedar Valley within Paphos Forest to the north west of the Troodos. It is a place renowned for thousands of Cyprus Cedars, a close cousin of the Lebanese Cedar. Leaving Troodos Square behind headed first for Kykkos near where Archbishop Makarious in buried in a tomb on Mount Throni by the monastery where he was a novice monk in the 1920's and 30's.

During other visits to the island had seen the results of the civil war between ethnic Greeks and ethnic Turks and heard many stories of the atrocities and behaviour of the local population, some very good, but some very bad. The rumbling of troubles started back in 1950. It was only a year since the civil war in Greece had ended and Greece was still a monarchy when Makarios became Archbishop of Cyprus at the age of 37. Cyprus was still under British rule and he was de facto leader of the Greek community on the island. Makarios soon became an advocate of Enosis, which was the term used for the union of Cyprus with Greece. Troubles began to develop such that by 1955 a Greek faction who had a more violent approach to Enosis through their organisation EOKA, (Ethnikí Orgánosis Kipriakoú Agónos, translated as, "National Organization of Cypriot Struggle"). Its leader was George Grivas an ex Greek soldier. The Greek government at the time wanted Cyprus to have self-determination and raised the issue at the United Nations. However, Cyprus, which wasn't fully Greek for there were Turks too. The British colonial government brought in new laws to suppress Enosis, but Makarios defied them. The insurgency became critical and Cyprus's governor was forced to arrest Makarios and have him exiled in the Seychelles. Around this time the Turkish community on Cyprus floated the idea of partition, Taksim and the dispute became increasingly polarised.

By 1958 the Greek government had abandoned the idea of Enosis and encouraged the British government to bring about Cyprus's independence. Makarios was invited to London to finalise the plan. By the end of 1959 Makarios was elected president of the newly formed independent Cyprus. This was fully realised on August 16th 1960. However, the constitution was a mess and caused critical ethnic tension.

By 1963 Makarios was forced to propose thirteen constitutional amendments, but the Turkish community viewed them as threatening their rights and Turks within office resigned their positions. The break up included the vice president and violence broke out once more.

In 1968 the military junta of colonels in Greece, who had come to power in 1967, created a new Greek constitution for the government in Athens. The result was a renewed support for people like Grivas to promote Enosis again. The result was many new terrorist attacks. The junta in Greece wanted to get rid of Makarios and forced him to purge his ministers who were against the junta. The pressure was compounded by the fact that officers in the Cyprus National Guard were full supporters of the junta being former Greek regulars.
It was in 1973 when a new junta had been established in Athens that Grivas's guerrilla tactics had evolved to an all-out civil war through the EOKA B paramilitaries, but these in the end were defeated by Makarios and Grivas's position became untenable and later Grivas died of a heart attack.

But there were still hardliners in EOKA and in 1974 with the Greek junta's help a Cypriot Greek coup d' etat was established in Nicosia catching Makarios's forces off guard. Fortunately, Makarios was rescued by the British and taken by helicopter to a British base and then flown off the island, as the Greek forces went on to control the whole island. A couple of weeks later Makarios addressed the UN Security Council denouncing the coup as a Greek government led action. Five hours after his address Turkey invaded the island taking the Greeks by surprise. They had the right to do this because under the original Treaty of Guarantee, Britain, Turkey and Greece were entitled to cooperate in order to intervene to restore the constitution of Cyprus. Having established that his administration was the rightful government of the whole island Makarios returned and worked hard to establish territorial integrity, but was thwarted by the Turkish occupation that remains to this day. Makarios died of a heart attack three years later on August 3rd 1977.

Returning to our travels, excitement began at Pendoulas where we found the road closed. It had a barrier across it. However, a sign said it was alright for vehicles less than two tons to proceed. Found the road onwards a little rough, as it had slipped, with repairs still in progress but saw no one working there. Continued onwards heading for Kykkos then Stavros toward the west, the road corniche like to Dôdeka Anémoi. There were steep drops to our right with extensive views of the north coast and to our left sheer cliff faces from which numerous rocks had fallen on to the road. By chance, although the driving was difficult at times there was no other traffic to bother us.

About an hour and a half later reached a parking area. In the mean-time the weather had deteriorated to gloomy cloud although in the far distance saw that the horizon to the north-east and west was clearly in sunshine.

It was about a quarter to eleven when we left the car to walk along a forest road to Mount Tripilos. It climbed steeply through sweetly scented pines, mostly Pinus Nigra, that have downward-facing cones. There were many other varieties of tree and bushes too, some of which had been flowering, but with the Cedars stood out. Cedrus Brevifolia is native to the Troodos and grows tall to around 20m. It has bright green to glaucous coloured needles, with erect sessile cones.

The road went through many convolutions as we progressed higher up the mountain. Through gaps in trees saw glimpses of surrounding mountains. It took us three quarters of an hour to reach the summit. Wooden tables and benches stood amongst trees for people to have seating for picnics, but it was silent. No other people were about, we were in the gloom by ourselves. The distance from the car park probably only 2km, but about 212m below us.

From the 'Look-Out' post looked out at distant Mount Olympus, magnificent with grey-white cloud covering its forested slopes. Northward saw sunlit mountains before Morphou Bay, the western most seaboard of the Turkish occupied zone. Decided to continue walking onwards for about an hour before turning back. Doing so hoped to reach the Cedar Valley picnic spot at an estimated distance of 2.5km and a descent of 200m.

It was about the same gradient as our ascent but the forest road turned and twisted even more with a big looping descent to the valley floor. Cedars grew around us, but it was taking us more time than we had estimated and were getting tired. Reaching yet another long hairpin turn gave ourselves another five minutes.

Plane trees, in their showy autumn colours, grew alongside cedars in a dry stream bed. As we were about to give up and turn back heard the sound of a car and decided to carry on. After another minute reached the picnic spot and a drivable road. One car followed another until at last were left in peace amongst the tall elegant cedars of the valley that claimed their pride of place within the thick forested mountains. A wild sheep known as the Cyprus Mouflon is said to roam the forest but saw no sign of them.

After having lunch at the picnic spot walked back to the car in good time. The climb up to Tripilos seemed easy. The walk had been enjoyable, but in the gloomy weather of low cloud the forest was a place for trees not humans.

The drive back was at first uneventful seeing only one car. Thinking about the animals seen or heard could only list a deer seen during the morning drive, and some birds, including jays, magpies and smaller unidentified birds heard in the forest, their music interrupting the otherwise quietness.

Reaching Kykkos found it crowded with coaches and cars, but passed through unhindered. Passed the road barriers at Pendoulas having had no trouble on the road and climbed towards Troodos. Had to switch on the car headlights as dark low cloud had swept in. The persistent mist cleared approaching Troodos square where we parked to find it more crowded that previous times. Kebab stalls were doing a roaring trade, but we strolled over to a guy selling hot chestnuts and bought a bag from him. While snacking on these browsed other stalls. Cicely wanted some cards, but found nothing suitable. Passing by another stall a guy offered me some brittle to taste and found it pleasant but didn't buy.

Drove down the mountain to Platres and the Petit Palais hotel. It was still busy with Sunday customers taking lunch in the restaurant. Had a coffee at the bar before retiring to our room to shower and rest before dinner.

Woke the next day to another lovely morning, blue sky stretching to the horizon. From our balcony looked out on the golden glow of glorious autumn colours displayed by trees down to the valley below. After breakfast drove up to Troodos, but from there headed towards Nicosia out of the high mountains to lower hills towards the plain progressing through farmland and poor looking villages. At Kato Koutrafas turned off the main road to go through the village to a narrow lane with farms on both sides, some with many tunnel cloches. After a short time reached the village of Nikitari where the now narrow road wove intricately through its centre. Old women wore colourful headscarves waved to us, as we went by. Old men sat in a line on a bench outside of the 'kafenion'. They stared at us while leaning heavily on their sticks.

Just after passing through Nikitari the narrow road joined a much wider one that took us through wooded countryside into foothills. Reaching the top end of a valley at an open area stopped and parked the car. Beyond low stone walls, in a grove of eucalyptus trees, stood the church of Panagia Asinou that is dedicated to the Virgin of Phorbia and is one of the UNESCO World Heritage Churches situated on the island.

An elderly man was repointing part the stone walls, whilst in the doorway stood another old man waiting to greet us. He had a little English for us to communicate, although it was a struggle. All the doors in the church were open to light up the ancient walls where a colourful display of twelve-century to seventeenth century Byzantine frescoes awaited our perusal.

The small yet wonderful church designed in two parts, a vaulted single aisle nave and a narthex that apparently is an add on completed in the twelve-century. The church was built in 1099 and used to be part of a monastery that was eventually abandoned at the end of the eighteenth century. Saw that there were little signs of any remains of monastic buildings outside, but noted that a steeply pitched tiled timber second roof protected the church building. Later found out that this was built in the twelve-century too.

Inside printed screens shielded the altar and beyond them stood golden objects on a cloth. However, these were overshadowed by the magnificent and wonderful pictographic display of religious images covering walls and ceiling, as well as the inside of the dome with no free space. We weren't allowed to take photographs, but bought a book that illustrated them.

We stared at the walls for a long time trying to decipher the messages and illustrated stories that the artists who painted them were trying to convey. It was obvious that a number of different artists were involved because of different styles in the portrayals and colour palettes were different too. Of course, the Virgin was displayed, and Christ, but also found St George and some Old Testament prophets. Many other saints, unknown to us, were also portrayed. The artistic assemblage was overwhelming and was well worth our visit.

The Haiku composed at the time,

Ancient images

Look down from old painted walls

Portray simple faith

The church stood in a prominent position at the head of the valley looking out towards the plain. From there headed back to Nikitari staying on the good road that went on to Vyzakia. Then turned back towards the hills and on towards Agia Marina. From Agia Marina drove on through thickly wooded country to Xyliatos. A short time afterwards passed by a dam in a forested valley to see a sign that indicated Stavros tou Agiasmati Church. Followed the indicted forest trail for a short while as it wound through woods. After driving a short distance along the difficult terrain spotted an old Venetian caravan bridge. Here it was too difficult to continue driving on and returned disappointed to the main road and drove on towards Lagoudera. When we reached the village took a road that indicated to Pangia tou Araka Church, 'Our Lady of the Pea'.

This large church and part of a monastery is one of the ten UNESCO World Heritage churches situated on Cyprus. It has outstanding murals. Found it located on the northeast slopes of Madari. Our guidebook gave us a little information but is given in italic below.

Most of the church's history is recorded within its mural paintings. From the inscription of the interior north lintel, it was stated that they were completed in December 1192. They were painted by a monk, trained in Constantinople, named Theodore Apsevdis. Apsevdis's work was possibly commissioned by a Byzantine aristocrat named Leontios Authentes, who was seeking refuge at a nearby monastery that was built by his father. Around the 14th century, the mural paintings had to be restored because of water damage. An inscription for these restorations is signed by a deacon named Leontios.

The church has a second roof covering as at Panagia Asinou and inside is a single aisle with frescos mainly at one end. Some of these had been covered by a lectern of finely carved wood. The outside walls are also partly covered by frescos and on the south eastern wall of the church is a lovely mural of the Virgin. This was painted in 1192 and across from it a mural of Saint Simeon holding Christ as a child with John the Baptist standing next to him.

The church stands in a fine position at the head of a wooded valley and from there drove back towards Lagoudera. Before reaching the village took a road to Livadia. Arriving in the village admired the wooden houses with balconies that were being restored. From there took a road to pass through Alithinou. Shortly after the village drove up a steeply rising narrow lane that wound up into the hills and after about 3km reached a church that nestled below us at the end of a metalled road.

Walking over to the church door found it closed. A notice stated telephone Mr Vasilis Hadjigeorgiou, at Platanistasa to visit. That place was nearby so set out to find him. Drove back down to the main road and on to his village that spread along a steep hillside. Stopped at what we thought was its centre and Cicely got out to ask a young woman with a small child leaving a café that she was closing up. She said that she would fetch Vasilis for us a strode quickly off up a village alley shouting his name. She returned to us saying that he would come to us shortly. We thanked her before she drove off.

Soon afterwards an old man appeared carrying a tank of fuel we assumed would be for a generator. He got into the car and we drove off back to the church. On arrival drove down a stony track to the place housing the generator. The old man got out and went inside to start up it up. Soon a loud engine noise indicated he had been successful. He emerged and directed us to the church saying that it was OK to take photographs.

Firstly, entered by an outer door to a corridor that surrounded the church before passing on through an inner doorway, then gasped in astonishment. It is a small church with a single aisle but all inside it is covered with wonderful and fabulous frescoes that illustrated biblical stories and stories of saints.

The old man began his tour with the aid of a bright light served by the generator that was held on a stand. He explained who the illustrated figures were and the story they told. We spent many minutes there with the charming old man full of church knowledge. He also explained the alter area and permitted me to enter. It was obviously a very old church with hand painted furnishings. The centre line down the aisle also had engraved illustrations. Back in the corridor saw that the outer walls of the church were also heavily decorated. Inside though the memorable illustrations for us were St Mamos and the marmalade lion and portrayals of St George and St Michael.

Discovered later more about Mamos. He was a devout Byzantine hermit who refused to pay income tax since as he logically pointed out he had no income other than small alms. The local Governor had him arrested, but as he was being escorted into custardy a lion (unknown in Cyprus) leapt from roadside bushes onto a lamb that was grazing peacefully nearby. Mamos commanded the lion to stop and picked up the lamb. He completed the journey to the capital by riding the lion. Sufficiently impressed the Governor exempted Mamos from paying taxes and ever since the Saint has enjoyed a fervent by tax evaders, a massively popular cult in the Hellenic World.

We bought a book about the World Heritage Sites and gave him four pounds, which seemed to please him and drove him home. On the way there though he insisted that we should stop to take a photograph of the church from high up, from there he pointed out Nicosia located in the far distant plain. Back at his village we thanked him again for his wonderful tour and left the way he had instructed us towards Troodos.

Reading more about the church, which we discovered is called Stavros tou Agiasmati, found out that the frescoes were completed in 1494 but with no date given for when the church was originally built. The book we bought states that the church has the most complete cycles of mural paintings of the second half of the fifteenth century. The name of the church is derived from spring or well near a church. The book also informs that there used to be a monastery for which the church was originally part of. Only a few ruins remain to the south of the church. It goes on to describe the architecture as a single aisled building with a steep pitched timber roof covered with flat tiles that extend beyond the main structure to form a portico on all four sides, a feature unique in Cyprus.

Drove on, following instructions, upwards out of the valley to Alona passing through its narrow alleys and by its vine bedecked village houses before leaving towards Polistipos. Soon left Polistipos behind and joined a main road to go on to Chandria and Kyperounter. The view of distant Mount Olympus quite spectacular. Cloud formations had bubbled up around it and whisps of white cloud descended as mist to move along the valley. Sunbeams that shone through it to Madhari and the ridge walk, gave it a magical touch. Climbing further found ourselves above the cloud with a clear blue sky above. Soon though descended through cloud again to Platres for a coffee at our hotel.

Cappuccinos with slices of honey and nut cake made a good ending to a tour of churches. Later that evening went down to the bar for a beer before dinner.

Woke the next day to yet another glorious morning. So romantic a light that you can never tire of and in the autumn especially pleasurable with its golden tones. Cicely said that we must go over to investigate hotel Rodon at Agros. This was built in the 1980's by locals as a cooperative. So, after breakfast set off down the valley towards Limassol. Shortly afterwards turned eastward towards a region called Pitsiliá. Passed by many farms and vineyards towards Pelendri to bypass the village that had one of the World Heritage churches nearby. The road followed the curve of the mountain before climbing once more to Potamitissa before taking the road to Agros. Had good views of the surrounding landscape from our high position. A fine agricultural area with nearby wooded mountains. Terraced hillsides with fruit orchards and vineyards illustrated its richness.

Agros came into view reaching the top of a hill. Found it nestling comfortably in a fold of the mountains at an elevation of around 1100m. It is famous for its roses, including the damask variety, and cured meats as well a growing and providing a range of fruit and vegetables. Hotel Rodan is located on a promontory overlooking steep slopes to an large open amphitheatre of terraced farms and lower hills. Drove on to the centre of the village and parked the car.

Nearby at a café enquired of a woman within whether there was a tourist office in the village. She said no but I might find information in the hotel. Left to stroll up the main street browsing the shop windows on the way to see if there was any honey for sale, for we had seen many bee hives on the morning drive. At a bend in the road two cafes were located opposite each other. Old gnarled male characters sat outside of each staring across the road at the others. Who knows what passed through their minds. Passed them by with a few stares but no comment. There was a lot of new building work going on as we had seen in other villages. Agros was no different seeing a cement mix pouring down tubes from a lorry that disappeared down a slope from the roadside. Bulldozers were parked nearby.

We had passed by several shops selling honey but all in plastic tubs, so didn't buy any and returned to the car to drive to the hotel. The hotel looked like a large international one with no homeliness, as at the Petit Palais. Went inside to reception where I enquired about local walks. The young man there showed me directions on a map that he had. It was much better than the one we had of a good circular walk. Thanking him took the more detailed map with us and returned to the car to change into our walking-gear.

It was around ten thirty when we set out the weather still perfect. Firstly, climbed steps leading from the main road onto a rough path. Pushed through weed like growth and summer baked grasses with wild flowers gone to seed. On the way stirred up many insects, including several large grasshoppers. One of these jumped high from surprise of our footfalls and hit my chest before rebounding back into the undergrowth. Saw many small orange butterflies that zipped around hither and thither and small lizards that scurried to their nearest burrows. At a group of pine trees, many more of which we had passed growing here and there on the hillside, found that the rough path led on to a narrow village road where a few houses were located. Followed this road northward to a fork where an arrow sign guided us to a course track that looped around terraces. In these many vines grew that were now in their bright autumnal colours. The track followed the contours of the hillside until another sign guided us to the proper footpath train on stony surface. Bushy plants grew alongside it and sometimes in the path.

The track meandered through the vine terraces and fruit and nut orchards too. Saw many cistus plants attractively bordering the trail. Soon the outlook changed to a mix of trees, mostly oaks and pine. Noted that the types of oak varied, as we had seen before, but some of the trees appeared larger and older and had even larger acorns than previously found on the island.

The vista to the south and west was idyllic, with far blue grey mountains and with a wide landscape of agricultural life of the Pitsiliá. Walking on the pines grew denser in a transition of garrigue to open woodland. Numerous wild flower seed heads indicated what a glorious show it must have been earlier in the year and identified amongst them alliums, asphodels, foot high muscaris and verbascums.

There were certainly more flowering plants than we had seen on previous walks and many butterflies flittered around too. Amongst these butterflies were the orange ones, coppers, clouded yellows and different blues that we couldn't identify. At one of the benches placed along the trail sat to admire the glorious view before progressing further. The trail ended at a rough forest track where we crossed to climb a hill with a radio mast and solar cells on top. From there looked down the valley to Potamitissa spread out across a hillside with its white walled red roofed houses glistening in the sunshine.

Returned to the track and followed it down to a road taking the direction towards Agros. Passed by a number of beehives listening to a loud murmur of bees buzzing around them. After walking a short distance took a narrow footpath that led through oaks and pines with a view to our right through the trees of Kato Milos, situated below us. Shortly afterwards the footpath merged with a farm track and turned to our right. After a short climb saw a church below us and went down to it to take a look. Found it to be an old church but unfortunately the doors to it were locked. Beyond it across a steep sided valley saw the village of Agios Ioannis nestling on the mountainside located below the 1554m peak of Papousta. Looking carefully spied another valley. White poplars spread along it, glinting golden in the sunlight.

Carried on around the hillside our senses now heightened and discovered another church, but again found it locked. Continued along the track descending towards a reservoir that showed evidence of drought with a low water level. Walked onwards to the dam and from there took another farm track that headed in a north easterly direction. Below us were numerous other tracks, cultivated terraces and farms. Fruit and nut trees grew in great numbers but to our left the hillside was covered in garrigue vegetation. A notice stated game reserve.

The track curved away from Agios Ioannis and across a valley gorge saw a road and shortly afterwards spotted Hotel Rodon in the distance. The track changed to a metalled narrow road. Soon reached a farm with both goats and sheep in housed wooden sheds their body perfumes wafting out with thick and unpleasant scents in the afternoon heat, much different to preferred pine resin smells experienced earlier. A spaniel followed us for a short way until distracted by another dog locked in a shed.

Passed by an agricultural centre on a steep slog up to a main road and joined it near to school buildings. From their walked along the road back to the hotel. I estimated that the height we had climbed upwards was around 150m and were glad to get back to the car where we change out of our walking gear.

Afterwards feeling in need of refreshments went into the hotel to the piano bar for a beer. Found the place empty except for one or two staff. After a rest and suitably refreshed drove the car down to Pelentri and parked next to a sign to the church. Strolled down a narrow concrete road that descended to the bottom end of the village in the valley. Passed by a number of roadside houses, where one of the gardens saw luscious hanging bunches of glossy black grapes. The road curved around to the church and then descended steeply to the valley bottom. The church has a prominent tower but has no false roof like the other World Heritage Churches we had entered.

I found the door was locked, but just as we decided to return to the car a man came striding towards us with a key. He opened the door, welcomed us and invited us inside. Found it similar to the others, but was built in three parts with two altar sections. Told it was a fourteenth church that is dedicated to the Holy Cross. The first impressions of the murals were not good. They were dark and in need of careful restoration, although some repairs and protective measures had been carried out. Yet found in one part that the wall and ceiling frescoes were exquisite and clear to see. It was obvious that the church didn't have the funds, as other churches, to look after its art. Discovered that that the murals were of the Palaiologan period that dated from the fourteenth century. Consulting our 'Rough Guide' read that the church was built by Timios Stavrou. According to the text is has a square floor plan and is divided into three aisles that are said to be unique in Cyprus. There is no narthex only a high dome supported by four columns. One of the illustrations was of the 'Tree of Jesse' that showing the genealogy of Jesus. There was also a fine silver cross on one of the altars depicting scenes from the stations of the cross, quite unusual and probably a church treasure.

Left the church to cloudy skies and drove back to Platres to take a stroll around the town admiring the fine houses, at the same time browsing shop windows and buying some wooden Christmas decorations.

Back at the hotel before dinner talked to madame about her lovely embroidery that she works on every winter. A table cloth she worked on had taken several winters, but yet to complete. What she had done so far was exquisite.

Dinner was a vegetable soup followed by the usual salad, then a main course of pork chops served with chips, peas and sliced carrots. Dessert was a large bowl of washed black grapes. Of course, we had the usual bottle of wine to drink with the meal, then a coffee for me before bed.

Woke next day to yet another fine morning although passed the middle of November it was such lovely weather. Later after a good breakfast walked up to the tourist office to enquire about the best route to see Venetian bridges. Shortly afterwards drove off towards Agios Nikolaos to go via Kato Platres and Mandria, as instructed. When we reached Mandria took a metalled road towards Agios Nikolaos. Had exceptionally fine views of the landscape ahead and saw to our right the deep wooded valley in which a walking trail and three bridges were to be found. These Venetian bridges were marked clearly on our map. The person in the Tourist office said that we would have to park the cat in Agios Nikolaos, but in the village spotted a sign to the Kelefos and Elaia Bridges and a metalled road that went in the direction of the sign.

The narrow road dropped steeply down towards the deep valley below. Initially passed through an open sun blest countryside full of vineyards with distant bare hills to the west. The drive down took us into pine woods and descended deeper into the valley before reaching a parking area near to a bridge. The bridge, named Tselefos, (Kelefos), is made of Roman style brick and has a single bow arch spanning the narrow sparkling river Diarizos. It's a very picturesque and peaceful site we found enclosed by idyllic autumn-coloured woods. A beautiful place to spend the whole day relaxing and dreaming of past Medieval times when the bridge was built.

A Haiku composed at the time,

Forgotten highway

Hides beneath its woodland cloak

Arched bridges still stand

Cyprus was once one of the Crusader States and controlled by the Lusignan dynasty. It was in 1468 that James II became king and chose the Venetian Catherine Comaro to be his wife. This was extremely pleasing to the

Venetian Republic as they had long had their eyes on the island for both commercial and trading rights. The marriage took place by proxy in 1468 when Catherine was only fourteen years old. James died of a sudden illness not long afterwards and Catherine who was then pregnant with his child became regent. However, her son died of malaria before his first birthday and in 1474 she became monarch.

The Island had been in decline for many years and paid tribute for protection to the Egyptian Mamluks. Yet on her ascent to the throne the Island was virtually controlled by Venetian merchants. She continued to rule until 1489 when she was forced to abdicate and sell the administration of Cyprus to the Venetian Republic. It is said that with tears in her eyes, she set off with her knights and ladies from Nicosia to end the last Crusader State. Nevertheless, Catherine was allowed to retain the title of Queen and was made sovereign Lady of Asolo in the Veneto. The Venetians controlled Cyprus until 1571 when the Ottoman Turks captured the island.

Cicely walked over the bridge and found on the other side in an area of damp ground with flowering white cyclamen that had reddish pink markings in the throats of the flowers. Nearby the river flowed fast and bubbled over massive boulders. Tried walking up the river but found the going tough and returned to the car to drive on to the next bridge.

Drove at first on a new metalled road that had been carved out of the hillside to leave quite a scar. It was only a short distance later that the road deteriorated to a rough forest trail that was signposted to Mylikouri. Had to park the car, as it became increasingly difficult to drive along the stony trail in out small car, then changed into our walking gear.

The trail headed up through a pine wood with the river gurgling below. After about a kilometre of walking came to a bridge, the 'Gefiri tis Elias'. It is a smaller bridge than Tselefos and is entirely made of stone. The river there was narrower but with steep sided banks, so the bridge required only a shorter span. Saw that maintenance work was being done to improve the access to the bridge. Walking over it found rough uneven cobbles at the centre of the span that were quite slippery. We surmised that these cobbles must have covered the whole roadway in the past. Found on the far side distinct signs of the old Venetian caravan route that ascended the hillside. Didn't follow this but instead walked along the river where we discovered growing in the moist ground masses of daisy like flowers. The stems were about 20cm long and emerged from rosettes of oblate leaves. Some of the petals had a rosy hue while others were white, I thought that must be Bellis Sylvestris. Its common name is Southern Daisy. There were cyclamen too growing there, coloured purple on the reverse side of the leaves with the usual mottled green on the topside. Its flowers were white with reddish colouration in the mouths, probably a Sowbread type. Also growing there were small violet pea like flowering plants. The plants were about 30cm in diameter with sage green leaves. It may have been Goats Rue, or Galega Officinalis.

Left botanising to climb up the riverside bank to the track and walked back to the bridge. Cicely had found a cyclamen that had been pulled from the ground. I discovered that it had some viable seeds and took a few with us to try out at home.

Spotted a bench situated on the hillside beneath trees and walked over to it to take a break. Nearby found Autumn Lady's Tresses orchids growing in number, Spiranthes Spiralis. Sat on the bench absorbing the delightful forested environment before later following the track uphill through pines to join a forest trail. Turned left on it and discovered growing nearby a yellow pea like flower similar in shape to the violet one found earlier, but they grew on spiky leafed stems. This plant we didn't identify.

Walked back to the car thinking that the place must be wonderful in spring and late summer with a wealth of different plants seen that were already forming their leaves.

Back at the car had to abandon the search for the final bridge to the west because the trail was undrivable in the car we had and decided instead to drive to Agios Ioannis to try and find access from there.

In the area there were many previous Turkish enclaves and as we drove through Agios Nikolaos stopped to look at an abandoned mosque. Its minaret was still in place, but its balustrade was rusting. The ground around it was weed strewn and a number of houses nearby abandoned and locked up. The Rough Guide informed us that the name of the Turkish enclave was Vrécha, but now called Vretsia and was abandoned in 1974. It had a UN Post, but was covered in graffiti proclaiming partition. Such a shame for it was once one of the most beautiful spots in the district with ample supplies of water and good land. Now it lies abandoned. The previous republic administration also never supplied them with electricity.

From a distance the hillside now looks bare and scarred. In our reading discovered that the former Turkish inhabitants at Agios Ioannis practiced the Linobambakoi faith. The word Linobambakoi is a combination of two Greek words *linen* and *cotton*. This of course refers to the dual character of the religious identity of the group who practiced a mixture of Muslim and Greek Orthodox rituals. They baptized and confirmed their children before Muslim circumcision. The children were given both Muslim and Christian names the latter being kept secret. In marriage they experienced both Muslim and Christian rites and continued to visit both the Mosque and the church. Even at death when they were given a Muslim burial they had consolations from the Christian church. Many of the people were of Venetian decent with names such as Mehmet Valentino.

A Haiku composed at the time,

Abandoned village

Forgotten friendships long past

Is there a future?

Trying to find a suitable route to the Roudias bridge wasn't successful and after a few ascents and descents decided to give up on the idea and head back east to Foini, a place notable for its pottery. At first the road was a little difficult due to the road's bad state of repair. On the way stopped at a taverna just before Mandria to have lunch. The proprietor was fond of flowers. The gardens around the scruffy looking place were a delight. There were also many pot plants such as Love-lies-Bleeding and Chrysanthemums. Took a beer each with a packet of potato crisps to snack on.

After the short break drove on again in glorious sunshine through Mandria and on to Kato Platres where to turn towards Foini and eventually descended steeply to the village off the main road. The narrow road wove through the sleepy village with little to see except for old men sitting outside of a Kafenion. It didn't seem worthwhile stopping and drove back towards Kato Platres and then west to Mandria. Driving onwards took a sharp hairpin turn off to Omodos eventually taking the village access road to park in the busy place.

The village's main street is stone paved and bordered by trees. Many tourist shops of many varieties and cafés too were located along it. Found it a very busy place for tourists so far experience in the Troodos. At the end of the street stands a seventeenth century monastery. Took steps down to it and passed through an archway into a square with a church and cloisters. The church was immaculate with a golden altar, a variety of icons and with highly polished and patinated wooden furniture.

Shortly afterwards left the church to wander through a maze of village streets and alleys. People beckoned us in to look at their goods as we passed by shops and stalls. Walked on to pass by a glass blowing workshop, some old traditional houses, a building with a fine Venetian looking arch, a building housing a wine press and some very large ceramic pots that could have been used for wine. Noticed dark skinned people with cheery smiles that we thought might be part of a large population of Tamils from Shri Lanka who had settled on the island.

Drove back to Platres via Mandria and as it was after four in the afternoon and had a coffee in the lounge at the hotel. Later at dinner had a ravioli starter followed by the usual salad and a main course of spiced pork served with French beans. This was followed by a dessert of vanilla ice cream with quince chips. Later chatted with madame over coffee discovering that her father came from Paphos, although she was born in Pano Platres. She also told us that she remembered the Turks in Agios Ioannis. She also said for any future visit that the best time to see flowers was in May to June, which was also a quiet time.

The next day woke again to another brilliant morning and after breakfast set off again to the other side of the mountain. Not a cloud in the sky as we passed by Troodos and headed at first for Pedoulas. Descended the slopes of the Marathasa valley to the upper reaches of the village that hugged the steep hillside, where sunshine reflected off both the golden leaves of white erect poplars and gnarled old plane trees. In the main street shops had stalls set up outside of them already busy. With the crowds of shoppers made slow progress down the street as we drove further through the village and headed for Moutoullas further down into the valley about four kilometres away. In Moutoullas saw very old Bedford buses still in use parked at the roadside. Drove on to Kalopanayiotis and at the village turned off down a narrow lane to a church, St John Lamadistis. The road wasn't good, more of a dirt track with stone chippings. It led us down to a tributary stream of the river fed by sulphur springs. Drove passed fine old houses that looked out from the steep hillside and reached a modern bridge that spanned the gorge of the Setrachos river leading to a monastery.

Drove on along a new stone road leading upwards towards buildings and met a man coming towards us in a car. He indicated that we should reverse into a courtyard outside of the church. He got out of his car and welcomed us with a smiling cheery face then walked off through an archway.

Left the car to look around the outside of the obviously restored fine old buildings that were constructed in both wood and stone. Approaching the rear of the buildings met the man we had seen earlier and greeted us again thinking us lost. He went on to tell us where to find the priest, who was watering some flowering plants in the courtyard.

The priest wore a long blue dress and had a fine head of hair with a long beard. He told us that he had been looking after all the churches in the village for the last forty years. The man, I can't remember his name, stayed with us and explained about the monastery that no longer functioned as one. The three churches that were built at different periods were housed under one huge wooden roof. He was very enthusiastic and told us many stories. By this time the priest went to sit at the entrance to the churches to read his newspaper. The man took note of this and told us to go in and that he would meet up with us later to show us the museum.

The priest got up and welcomed us, as we entered the church complex. Inside it was awe-inspiring as with the other Byzantine churches seen. The first church was covered with murals, some looking very old and was perhaps the oldest of the churches dating from the eleventh century. The priest explained the details within the frescoes with a knowledgeable enthusiasm, but his English accent was hard to understand at times, so some of his explanations were lost to us. He took us one by one through the churches that appeared as one. The far one, the newest, was a Latin Chapel that had little light penetrating its inner sanctum. The frescoes, of sixteenth century origin, were Venetian so that more realistic figures were portrayed. The priest left us to look around further. Cicely showed me a mural she had discovered of kings fleeing on horseback.

Before leaving I donated some money to the churches and saw that the priest turned his back whilst I was doing this and continued to read his newspaper. Outside the man who had been with us earlier was there to pick us up. While Cicely delayed looking at the flowers in the courtyard the man took me over to a wall overlooking the valley. He told me the story of St Mark and Barnabus who had left Palestine for Cyprus. First, they had visited

Salamis, but also came to our location guided by a man who was to become the first bishop of Cyprus. The reason given for their visit was because of the curing spring waters and for baptisms. Cicely arrived, as he was telling me about the restoration of the museum building, which cost. 350,000 Cyprus pounds. It used to be a school building and is dedicated to a bishop. The basement of the museum houses icons from the monastery and surrounding churches that had fallen into a ruinous state.

Inside found it well air-conditioned. Sounds of religious music played in the background. The man, went on to explain the making of icons from structure to artwork. Some of the finest ones were shown in London in 2001. One of a Madonna with baby Jesus had eyes that followed you wherever you placed yourself with respect to it. There were several long rectangular icons saved from one church and an altar screen from another. The man was so enthusiastic showing them to us and pleased with our response. We thanked him and left to look at the bridge crossing the gorge. At a café later found the priest and the man drinking coffee together.

Returned to Pedoulas after a coffee break to drive along another narrow lane a little bit better than the way we had driven in. Cicely wanted to buy some honey so looked around the shops to find what she wanted. Later walked on to another World Heritage Church, Archangelos. It is a small church and by far the smallest of the six seen. In the silent inside an old woman dressed in black sat quietly. Found the murals dark and in poor shape. Some were on outside walls by the entrance and under its sloping roof. Didn't stay long, but as we exited a man with a stick beckoned us over to a museum, called the Byzantine Museum.

It wasn't a patch on one we had seen earlier on the day. It had new icons on show and not so old bibles. What made it worse was that the old man instructed us to donate money. He told us how much to give him even though he had told us nothing. There are always bad pennies around in any place that let a village down.

Stopped briefly in the village to shop before driving back to Platres. It had been very sunny with clear skies before droving over the mountain to enter cloud. Cicadas had been singing on the north side but at Platres it was cool and grey. After parking the car changed into our walking gear and set off for Millomeris Waterfalls.

A rough stone path led us down to a stream that rapidly flowed through a boulder strewn wooded valley. The trees a mixture of evergreen and deciduous, in particular plane trees and pine. Crossed by stepping stones to the other side to follow a track bordering the water before climbing up a hillside to the edge of a cliff. Heard loud sounds from rushing water coming from somewhere down the steep sloped valley but didn't see anything. The path continued uphill before it descended by steps to a rough stone roadway. Crossed the road to a concrete roadway that led us to a stone surface area with a 'No Through Road' sign. Three workmen there though waved us on through to a path leading to the Falls. Steps eventually led down to a narrow gorge in which the stream flowed. Crossed it by a narrow wooden bridge to a path that led us to a spectacular single drop waterfall.

By the pool beneath grew old gnarled plane trees with their roots down in the water.

Stayed for a while in this tranquil place before returning to the car. Back in Platres both of us felt exhausted from our effort and went into the hotel bar for a drink. I felt hot and sticky and left Cicely there to go to our room for a refreshing shower. A little later feeling much better joined Cicely in the bar for beer and some nuts.

Dinner that evening started with a leek soup followed by the usual salad, then a main course of moussaka. The red wine flowed well, as it was our last night there. A dessert of a honey and nut roll with coffee finished the evening well.

After breakfast the next day settled our account with madame and thanked her for an excellent stay. Platres had been an excellent base to explore the Troodos, surrounding villages and countryside. We had been blessed with magnificent weather and come to love the area that has so much to offer. It had been a glorious stay and began to appreciate its history, ancient and modern, and the suffering of its people. Although the botanical treats were good perhaps Maytime you would experience the true flowering of the island.

Drove off over the mountain, the temperature in Troodos was six degrees centigrade. Drove by way of Pedoulas seeing the mountains of Turkish zone clear and sharp. The weather fine although cold at altitude. Descended through foothills to Kykkos and wound down to the coast at Pomas the temperature risen to the middle twenties and the sky a clear blue. Headed west along the coast with a strong breeze causing white horses out at sea. Soon reached Polis and headed for the Aphrodite Hotel in the Akamas Peninsula which was to be our next walking base.

View from Balcony of Room at Petite Palace Hotel, Pano Platres

Kalidonia Falls

A View from the Atlanta Trail around Mount Olympus

Looking North from Adelfi Peak

View of Mount Olympus from Tripolos

UNESCO World Heritage Church - Panagia Asinou dedicated to the
Virgin of Phorbia

UNESCO World Heritage Church – part of monastery, Pangia tou Araka Church, 'Our Lady of the Pea'

UNESCO World Heritage Church – Stavros tou Agiasmati

Saint Mamos

View from Hotel Rodan of Agios Ioannis

Venetian Bridge - Tselefos, (Kelefos)

Venetian Bridge - Gefiri tis Elias

An Old Bedford Bus still in use near Moutoullas

UNESCO World Heritage Church – Monastery Complex and Church,
St John Lamadistis

Madonna and Birth of Jesus Mural

UNESCO World Heritage Church – Church of Archangelos Pedoulas

Emma Pap in the Székely Zone of Romania

Drove eastward from the 'Saxon' area of Romania, leaving beautiful Sighişoara, to pass through Securesc where at the roadside woven baskets were displayed for sale. Had planned the route as carefully as possible, but without detailed maps expected some interesting diversions. Told Roger to take a road that looked to be a short cut that was not on my route map. It took us off the beaten track through an attractive part of the countryside passing through the small village of Cobăteşti. Village names weren't the same as on my map, for they were all in Hungarian. It was like driving through a strange country, for this was Székely country, Harghita County.

The Székely people are among the oldest cultures to inhabit the Carpathian Basin. The origin of the Székelys is fascinating, but at the same time a matter of some historical controversy. Traditional scholarly accounts of the Székely origins state that they were Huns, who later adopted the Hungarian language (Magyar). Other scholars believe that the Székelys were a contingent of Hungarians that accompanied Attila to the Carpathian Basin. Some recent archaeological finds amongst the Ugar people in Eastern Turkestan seem to give some credence to the ancient Magyar legends. They state that the Magyars are direct descendants of the Huns. Yet the local people have many legends about their own origin. They believe that after Attila died and his empire disintegrated, Attila's youngest and favourite son Ernak (Prince Csaba), led them to safety in Transylvania before he returned to the east. Ernak did indeed take the main body of Huns back to Scythia, but to a region between the Black Sea and Caspian Sea. This is where the remaining Hunnic peoples, merged with the ancestors of the Magyars. This Hun-Magyar connection is also remembered in one of the famous Hungarian folk tales, 'The Legend of the White Stag'.

The legend describes how the two sons of Nimrod, Hunor and Magor, chased a white stag into a new land where they married daughters of the king. The descendants of Hunor became the Huns, while the descendants of Magor became the Magyars.

Eventually drove northwards through heavily wooded country with many horses and carts on the road too. This slowed us down to their gentle pace, as a consequence, Roger, the driver, became frustrated. Nevertheless, it wasn't long before we reached Korund where roadside stalls and shops sold ceramics, as well as trading in traditional costumes, carpets and woven baskets. It was a prosperous looking artisan place.

Korund potters are best known for their famous blue-and-white designs, which they have been creating since the 1700s. The main products are pots, pans, vases, candleholders, and cups. On display were beautifully decorated ornamental plates with a variety of symbols, such as wedge shapes, peafowl eye, and chessboard patterns. There is a saying in Korund,

"*Since the world existed, they have always produced pottery*". The Szkéler women say, '*The best corn porridge can only be made in vessels made in Korund*'.

Both Cicely and Linda browsed the shops and stalls, each buying examples of the Blue and White designs that included both animals and flowers. There was no time to linger though as we had a long drive ahead.

Drove off northwards again via Plaid and in due course along a country road that climbed eastward through thickly wooded terrain, our destination still 50km away. It was a rough ride crossing hills and going through a pass at 1287m for the state of the road was appalling. It had many potholes and considerable damage from road slippage. It was after five o'clock when we eventually reached the town of Gheorgheni.

The hotels, or indeed the town, didn't look appealing to us so drove northwards again along the road to Toplița hoping to find accommodation in the village of Lăzarea, (Gyergyoószárhegy in Hungarian). Our guidebook showed 20 Pensiunes, but on arrival a short time later saw no evidence of any. Thinking of nothing better parked in the centre of the small village.

Nearby a large village map was displayed on a notice board. We found it next to useless, for it was no help to us at all. All we could determine was that a castle stood on a hill close by. Fortunately, we had some telephone numbers. Roger tried one but got no response. Happily, a second number yielded a reply, as we were beginning to contemplate driving on to the next place that was a considerable distance away and it was getting late in the afternoon.

The woman who answered had no English, so Roger handed the phone to me whispering she speaks French. I don't know whether Roger thought I spoke fluent French, but I did understand some of what she was telling me. She was trying to describe how to get to her place from where we were and was very helpful and amiable. The instructions seemed quite complicated. These involved turning back towards Gheorgheni and with some left and rights and then to finish off down a lane. She sensed my difficulties understanding the instructions and said that her son spoke English, but was working up at the castle, but would get back to us. She did say something though about attending to it too.

I discussed the instructions with Roger and were considering how to follow them, not clearly knowing our starting place. Just as we were about to drive off, Madame turned up on a bicycle pedaling fast. I got out of the car to greet her when she said, "*suivez-moi*" waving her arms and smiling broadly, an attractive young woman exuding charm.

Roger drove off, slowly following the bicycle back along the main road before turning off down a narrow stony track. This led to her pensiune, that is named after her, 'Emma Pap'. Surprisingly found it to be a bungalow. Leaving the car entered the grounds through a double wooden side gate that led to a patio area. The grounds are long and narrow with outhouses strung out down one side.

Emma Pap welcomed us again with a captivating smile and beckoned us in to her small house. She showed us two double bedrooms that smelled strongly of mothballs. They were cluttered with personal objects, such as photographs and ornaments, just as in my grandmother's day. The entrance to one of the bedrooms was off the hallway while the other was off a small kitchen diner from where a concertina door led to a shower and toilet room. Emma, we found was both pleasant kind and although the price she charged wasn't cheap took the rooms, ours being off the hall and Roger and Linda's off the kitchen.

After the agreement she opened the main gates for Roger to drive the car in and closed the gates behind him. After putting our bags in the rooms, we assembled in the kitchen where Emma still smiling placed a small carafe of Pálinka (an alcoholic bilberry drink) on the table with four glasses and asked us what time we would like dinner and breakfast.

I understood from her that the village was entirely made up of Székely people. She went on to say that for dinner there would be for the main course, a mushroom pasta dish, following soup and asked if this was OK. We agreed and went back to our rooms to sort out our cases and open windows to let in some fresh air. A little later all gathered again to finish off our drinks at a bench in the garden, which was situated alongside one of the outhouses. During our activities Emma had been shopping, going off on her bicycle and had come back with a bag of groceries and went into one of the outhouses to cook the meal. She had also asked us whether we would like wine with the meal, of course we said yes and she then disappeared into another outhouse to go down some steps, which we imagined to be a cellar, to fetch a bottle.

Dinner was ready on time at seven thirty as promised. She called us in to her small diner where the table was attractively laid. The soup proved to be excellent with thin strands of pasta floating in it. The main course was thick slices of pork cooked in a mushroom sauce and served with macaroni. For dessert she served us slices of cake. With the meal drank from a good bottle of red Swabian wine, possibly from the Banat region, or near to the Danube wine growing area.

After thanking her for such a fine meal sat outside on the bench again watching a glorious sunset staying there for some time in the warm air as darkness came. Later retired to our rooms, it had been a long day

Woke the next day to another glorious morning, Emma, who must have been sleeping in the single room next to ours, had laid out a fine breakfast of slices of salami, cheese, tomato and a paste with some bread. She also asked if we would like omletă. Of course, we all said, yes please, as expected though the omletă was scrambled egg. I had it with slices of good beefy tomatoes. During breakfast she asked if we were driving on to Gheorgheni, I said yes then on through Bicaz Gorges.

"Pourriez-vous me déposer quelquepar s'il-vous-plait?"

I turned to Roger and said Emma would like a lift to Georgheni. We agreed that this would be OK and left to get the bags.

Before I loaded the bags into the car, I looked through the 'Visitors Book'. It had comments from 2008. We were the first English people to stay in that period and I wrote my comment for our stay. Looking through the other comments there was an amusing one from a Danish cyclist who wrote in English,

'Thank you for coming after me!'

It had been just a short stay with Emma, but was enjoyable and was a pity that we had no time to explore the village further for we had a long drive to the 'Painted Churches' in Bukuvina. For those who would like to come after us the village name means 'Bold Mountain'. It is famous for its castle. The village is closely entwined with the Lázár family. The castle was built in the fifteenth century taking place over a period of nearly eighty years. Later in the seventeenth century the castle was converted and expanded to a Renaissance defensive manor house being an important military and administrative centre in Székely Lands.

A historical story that I picked up at Emma's relates to an event in 1658 when a group of Széklers, led by a student named Gábor Székely, defeated an invading Tatar and Moldovan army. In 1908 this battle was commemorated by a memorial plaque. A hill below the village is called

Tatarhill and is the place where those enemies killed in the battle are buried.

After putting our cases in the car boot Roger drove out of the gate. It turned out that Emma wanted to be dropped off at the hospital in the town centre, which was on our way. On arrival at Gheorgheni hospital we said our *'good byes and thanks'* to Emma Pap and left the town along a tortuous road, either side dark steep wooded hillsides of conifers.

One of the many carts on the road

Cicely and Linda at dinner at Emma Pap's

A young Emma Pap

A Short Trip to Ürgüp passing by Citadel Rocks in Cappadocia

Under a sky, almost deep sea-like blue, drove towards the Citadel Rock at Uçhisar in Cappadocia Turkey, a large rock structure riddled with caves. It was in the autumn of 2009 when we parked the car outside the entrance. Nearby, market stalls displayed colourful arrays of various dried berry fruits and nuts. Flocks of sparrows descended upon them prompting stall owners to draw nets over their produce and at times having to beat them off.

The 60m high rock tower stretch skywards before us. Most of its interior rooms and passageways are now blocked, yet in former times the rock served many purposes from Hittite times to those of Byzantium when perhaps 1000 people lived within it. In the past it contained cloisters, as well as residential areas.

After paying a fee entered a large cave and passed through it to an exit hole to climb steps. Walked on keeping to the outside of the rock, not attempting to enter any of the interior rooms and eventually climbed to the topmost part of the rock. From there the panoramic view of the valley down to Göreme was magnificent. Fairy chimneys and houses all blended in to the dusty landscape. To the northeast horizon the ominous misty grey volcanic cone of Erciyes Dagi rose upwards.

Erciyes Dagi, also known as Argaeus, is a large stratovolcano 3917m in height. In a small flat area, there were signs of old Byzantine grave cuts. A swallowtail butterfly landed, a gorgeous creature, but one of its tails was missing. We rested on top digesting all that was to be seen before descending to the car.

Drove off towards Ortahisar, going by a different route via 'Pigeon Valley', in which local villagers breed pigeons. The birds roost in man-made holes cut into conical rocks and cliff faces and farmers collect their droppings as guano fertiliser. Carried on along a wide road from Nevesehir towards Ürgüp to eventually turn down a narrow lane to Ortahisar and came across a viewing terrace that overlooked the Citadel Rock.

The Citadel like at Uçhisar was used as a defensive position as well as a troglodyte settlement. At its base typical old houses skirted it, blended to the colouration of the Rock. The 'Rough Guide' informed us that the sides of the valley are littered with caves that are used for storage purposes, typically for apples, potatoes and any imports, such as oranges and lemons transported from the country's Mediterranean shores. From our position people on the Citadel looked the size of ants, some seen right on top. It is a magnificent sight, a perfect composition, with the minaret of a mosque to its left as well as the far blue-grey mass of high Erciyes Dagi.

Drove on once more heading towards Ürgüp, the largest town in the area. Parked the car in a small central square and headed over to a raised terraced area built over shops where tables and chairs were set outside of a café-bar. There ordered Coca-Cola and sat for a while looking at our surroundings and deciding what to do. Roger wanted to visit the Haman that was situated close by and the girls wanted to look at the shops, so I decided to just stroll around the town to look what it had to offer. We agreed to meet up at the car in an hour's time.

I strolled up the main road to look at Ürgüp's Citadel. It wasn't as impressive as the others seen and the caves looked as if they were used mostly for storage, at least at the lower level. I turned back to the square then walked down Ataturk Boulevard where there were many shops and soon spotted Linda and Cicely in a shop selling spices and many other colourful items. I pressed on down the road and looked into a window that displayed Turkish art and paintings. The shop's owner stood in the doorway leaning on a doorpost. He asked if I liked art and I replied in the affirmative. We carried on chatting, he obviously liked to practice his English. After a while he asked me if I would like to look at his stock and have some tea. I declined gracefully and said that my wife who was in shops behind me might want to do so later. Said my goodbyes and carried on downhill passing by further shops and came to a bronze statue, which was dedicated in 2005. It was of a man and woman carrying a large basket of grapes between them. Obviously, it depicted the grape harvest and was located in a small park-like area outside of a museum.

Outside of the town had seen some wineries for Cappadocia is a centre of wine production and local produce contained in barrels is stored in caves within the town. Although the region produces both good red and white wine, which is a good source of income, few locals consume it. Turkey, being an Islamic country at heart remains a very low consumer of wine compared to the

Western World. Droughts though have been a recent problem for grape growers and grapes baking in very hot weather have often led to ruined harvests. However, new grape varieties and a better viniculture are having an impact for a better future. Medals have been won on the international scene and wine from Cappadocia is renowned for its distinctive flavours. Workers in viniculture get paid 12YTL for a twelve-hour day and welcome the opportunity that wine production gives them to make a living.

I carried on walking and came across three statues obviously representing Christian monks, or in one case a nun. They looked new and modern in design so probably didn't date from before the forced Greek exodus in 1923. These Turkish Greeks spoke their own dialect of Greek descending from Byzantine times. I was perplexed for there was no attribution, or dedication shown. Crossing the road, I intended to make a circular tour and walked down the road opposite. A new mosque constructed in local stone, Duayeri Camii, was dedicated in 1976 according to a sign seen over an impressively decorated gateway, gleamed in the afternoon sunshine. Away from the shops and cafés I turned back towards the town centre and came to a bazaar and café-bar area that was situated in a narrow open clean looking street. There men sat at tables outside of bars drinking tea and playing games. Some of the games I recognised, such as backgammon, draughts, and cards but one or two others involved brick like pieces as dominoes, but had pictures instead of dots; I couldn't fathom it out. When I passed one such table I was questioned and asked to sit and take tea, again I believed they liked to practice their English. So polite and charming they were I bowed thanked them, but declined and carried on until I came across another table surrounded by colourful men some with highly weathered faces. I would have liked to take a photograph, but they said no, nevertheless they talked to me especially one who had good English and asked me what I had seen in Turkey. He seemed pleased with my response and told me many other things that I must see before I leave. It seemed strange to him that an Englishman was in Ürgüp, he told me that the English generally confined themselves to the coast where many had even taken up permanent residence. I took my leave of them and headed into a square surrounded by shops and restaurants. Being a little thirsty I went into one and took tea inside and had a baklava too. The waiter had a little English but welcomed me and helped me choose the baklava from an ample selection of different types during which locals came in to buy sweetmeats, as well as cakes to take away. The schools had just turned out and in the café some of the mothers were with their offspring's sipping tea.

I still had plenty of time before I needed to return to the car and walked away from the centre again towards another of the town's hills. This time walked through a poorer quarter with smaller shops selling fewer goods. Coming down the street towards me were a young woman wearing a colourful hijab and long buttoned up coat holding the hand of a young girl. She was about ten and wore a school uniform. They both gave me beautiful smiles and before I could pass them the little girl asked me my name in very precise English. I told her and asked her name. She told me it was Gonja. Her mother smiled at me very pleased with her daughter's English skills, as I carried on the conversation asking her age and where she lived. The answer to the last question was difficult to interpret. We departed with smiles all round and waves of the hand.

It wasn't the first time that I was exposed to the amazing children in Turkey. A few days previous whilst wandering the dusty lanes through the cave like houses of Göreme had my first experience. We peered over a wall to a yard where a lop-eared sheep emerged from a rock cave to look at us. Across the way from there four young children, two boys and two girls, probably aged seven to eleven, sat on a wall that surrounded a rough looking stable yard. Two fine horses were penned within it with free ranging long legged scrawny chickens that looked like fighting cocks. They hopped on to the walls and into the yard. One of the children, a young girl, came up to me. She was possibly the eldest and wore a pink cardigan with an embroidered heart over a pale green sweatshirt and also wore short red trousers. She had an attractive face and very black shiny hair that was elaborately arranged in side and back bunches. "Hello, how are you?" she said in good accented English. I replied, "OK. How are you?" She replied, "I am OK too". I then asked what age she was. She thought about it, trying to remember English numbers I think, but one of the lads came up in the meantime. He had a cheeky round face with combed forward short black hair and wore a fun green sweatshirt with long black sleeves. The design on the front of the shirt was obviously taken from some cartoon character called 'Bad Boy' and was labelled 'Streets Sports'. He chirruped in, "ten!" And so it was that we all laughed together before saying goodbye to each other, the other girl raising her hand in high fives as a departing gesture.

I felt encouraged by the innocence of the children, free to play and converse as they wished. Also, their schooling must be good, as their English at such an early age would put our school kids to shame.

Back in Ürgüp carried on a little way before returning to the square where the car was parked. No one was there so I crossed the road to shops situated under the terrace where we had had our drinks earlier. Just as I reached the pavement a bride and groom got out of a car. Seeing me with a camera the bride asked if I would like to photograph them. I said yes of course and as I was taking it Roger arrived and shortly afterwards the girls too.

Rock Citadel Uçhisar from Göreme

Roger on top of Rock Citadel at Uçhisar

Rock Citadel Ortahisar, Background to its left the volcano Erciyes Dagi

Rock Citadel Ürgüp from Square

Children encountered at Göreme

Bride and Groom at Ürgüp

Environs of Agrigento and the valley of the Temples

It was in the September of 2010 that we headed south from Palermo in Sicily up into hills via the Eleutero valley. Then drove over into the Milicia valley bypassing towns such as Bolognetta and Villafrati where an attractive ruined castle, Castello Di Ce, stood out silhouetted against a grey skyline heavy with cloud. Went on through numerous villages, some showing evidence of recent forest fires with burnt trees right up to many of the houses. The surrounding hills became higher, some with peaks rising up to 1500m. Eventually drove down into another valley through which the river Vicari flowed and crossed over it to a tributary river valley before heading up it to Regalgioffolio.

Bypassed the town, but soon passed into another regional administration area when the road number changed. Hills brown and burnt were passed in a flash, as I was thinking about better weather for the sky had lightened to the south. It promised good things to come. Drove onwards into welcome greens with plantations, orchards with all kinds of agricultural produce. Saw melons being gathered in the fields.

Farming became more intensive, as we followed the Platani River downwards and patches of blue sky became more obvious. Even so dark clouds still swept in from the west. Stopped briefly at a restaurant outside of Agrigento to have a light lunch and a drink.

Back in the car I had detailed instructions of how to get to our accommodation for our stay in the area and began to navigate from them. Didn't have to enter the town of Agrigento, which spread out on a hill before us lit up in sunshine. Took a turn off down a ramp indicating to Porto Empedocle to join a valley road towards Raffadali. After only a few kilometers Roger spotted perched on a small hill above the road the Agriturismo and turned to drive up a stony track to a parking area outside of the Reggia Saracena.

Reggia Saracena is an old farmhouse completely renovated in Mediterranean style, surrounded by a lush yet quirky garden. It had within it a number of different statues of goddesses and lions and so on. Walked up steps to it where Giuseppe greeted us. He sat us down at a table in the garden and fetched us cool coca cola to drink. It was a good beginning, but were soon disappointed when he informed us that we could stay only for one night. We had changed our arrival date by a day just before we left the UK but had been expecting to stay for two nights. He went on to say we would be staying the second night at his place further up the valley, just a few kilometers away, and would still be able to eat in the restaurant, at least for dinner. After finishing our drinks, he fetched the keys and showed us to our rooms.

Roger and Linda were on the upper floor accessed by stairs from the garden situated close to the door of our room. The rooms were pleasant and had en-suite facilities. Once the bags were in the rooms and had a short rest decided, as dinner wouldn't be served until eight thirty, to make a preliminary visit to 'The Valley of the Temples'. It was close by, only a ten-minute drive away.

Roger had obtained verbal instructions of how to get to the Temples, but it soon became apparent that something was wrong. We had headed first in completely the wrong direction and after passing through a tunnel turned back guessing instead to head towards the sea. There was still no sign of the temples, or any sign directing us to them. It was quite a way west of Agrigento when Roger pulled in to a service station to ask for directions.

Headed back east following signs to Catania until saw a road sign directing us to the Temples. Next it was finding a place to park the car having missed a sign on the way up the hill towards Agrigento. Roger managed to turn around at the museum car park and drove back down hill to a roadside hut displaying cards and advertising information. I went in to get some instructions. The car park was further down located off a roundabout. It was there that we had missed the sign to the car park.

It was five thirty, as we crossed the road to the ticket office, after parking the car in a large sandy space. There discovered that last entry was at six thirty so had some time for exploration and told that tickets were valid the next day.

Exploring parts of Magna Graecia, had always been our intention whilst in Sicily. The name was given by Romans for the coastal areas of southern Italy. Settlers began arriving there from Greece as early as the eighth century BCE and brought with them a Hellenic culture and civilisation that left an imprint even in Roman times.

During the golden age of ancient Greece Agrigento was one of the leading cities of Magna Graecia. Estimates of the population at its peak before 406 BCE range up to eight hundred thousand.

Good light from late afternoon sunshine didn't last long before cloud drifted in again. The first temple ruin encountered was the former Temple of Castor and Pollux. In parts there was a large area of reddish fallen masonry that showed two courses of a wall. A picturesque and poignant part of the ruin is in one corner where three standing Doric columns are still in place with large stone courses on top of the columns giving an impression of a corner to the temple. Cypress Sempervirens trees bordered part of the site adding to its picturesque attraction.

Climbing, walked further on following a well-worn path towards the ridge where further temple ruins are located. Reading a little of the history given to us in a pamphlet I found out that it dates from 580 BCE when colonists arrived from Gela situated further along the coast. The place, was called by them Akragas. It is built on a plateau overlooking the sea with two nearby rivers, the Hypsas and the Akragas. A ridge that runs in a northerly direction offered them a degree of natural fortification and a high point for temples. In time Akragas grew, becoming one of the richest and most famous of the Greek colonies of Magna Graecia. In 406 BCE Carthaginians sacked the city and it never fully recovered its former status.

By 210 BCE Romans had capture the city and renamed it Agrigentum, nevertheless it remained a Greek speaking community for many centuries later. It became prosperous again under Roman rule and following the death of Julius Caesar in 44 BCE its inhabitants received full Roman citizenship. After the collapse of the Roman Empire the city passed through the hands of Ostrogoth's and Byzantines. Continued raids by Saracens forced the city to pull back its boundaries and use the former acropolis on top of the hill. Inevitably in 828 AD the Saracens captured the remnant city and renamed it Kerkent. This Arabic name was eventually Sicilianised as Girenti and retained this name until as recently as 1927 when Mussolini reintroduced an Italianized version of the Latin name, hence Agrigento. Today though on a per capita income basis it is now one of the poorest towns in Italy and has a long-standing problem with organized crime, particularly involving the Mafia and smuggling of illegal drugs.

This may give a little colour to the place and speculative thought about the Mafia, but why 'The Valley of the Temples'. Of course, it's a misnomer as it is on a ridge not in a valley where the temples are located. Apparently in the large sacred area to the south side of the ancient city seven monumental Greek Doric style temples were constructed during the period of 6th and 5th centuries BCE. Through archeological excavations and reconstructive work, they are said to constitute some of the largest and best-preserved ancient Greek buildings outside of Greece.

A path took us up towards a grove of trees where a large stonewall outlined a platform. Climbing up to it via a narrow dirt path I found not much left of the Temple of Olympian Zeus except for large blocks of scattered stone and two large prostrate figures. The size of the site though is very impressive. Some say that the temple was one of the largest in ancient Greece measuring at the base, on which I stood, 113.2m by 56m and that is about the same size as a football pitch today. The fallen figures I saw are called Telamones or Atlantes. They measure in height (or length on the ground) 7.61m. Originally, they were part of the structure and stood on plinths half the height of the walls and together with interspersed columns supported the weight of the heavy trabeation (a form of architecture that uses beams as supports rather than vaults or arches) on their raised arms.

Light was failing fast as we pressed further on up the ridge to the next temple, but before doing so watched a beautiful young woman, wearing a long pink ancient style Grecian dress, pick her way through fallen debris. The apparition wasn't a ghost of the past, but some gorgeous visitor to the site.

The next temple, after crossing the road up towards Agrigento, is named Concordia and is the best preserved on site. It has wonderful proportions of classic design and further on up the ridge the ruins of the last temple were outlined against the skyline. This was the temple of Hera Lacinia.

I caught up with Linda and together walked back to the road. Cicely and Roger though had gone off to look at the ruins of the temple of Hercules, whose remaining columns were seen sticking up above some trees.

Roger had the tickets so we had to wait at the turnstiles until they arrived. Shortly afterwards all gathered together again passed through the turnstiles into the first part of the walk up the ridge and walked back down to where the car was parked. The sun, still occasionally appearing through cloud, was setting and illuminated the landscape with a golden red glow. We planned to return in the morning to see the far temples in more detail.

It was just after seven when we left the site driving uphill towards Agrigento, passing by the museum. Found the town centre locked up with traffic due to some slight collision between two cars. It was a long wait, but eventually drove out of town in the direction of Palermo. Roger obviously frustrated by the delay missed the turn off ramp and had to drive on until we found a place to do a U-turn. It was quite dark when we got back to Reggia Saracena at a quarter to eight. Consequently, it was a rush to clean up for dinner by eight thirty but made it on time joining Roger and Linda at our table.

The evening proved enjoyable with wine and conversation flowing throughout. A five-course meal added to the pleasure. Started with bruschetta, followed by four different plates of antipasto, a primo of pasta with a cheese sauce, a secondo of fried chicken, sausage and potatoes and finally a fruit bowl with watermelon, melon, peaches and grapes. With the meal we drank a luscious red Sicilian wine and with coffee the girls had a limoncello and Roger surpassed himself again with a large glass of sambucco.

It had been a good day particularly at the temples and I realized that I had to read more about the ancient city to find out about its people and their customs.

The next day arrived with a change of weather, a fine morning, the sky clear and bright. I went for a walk around the buildings meeting up with Giuseppe and the cook on the way. To one side, away from the main road, a stony track was bordered by masses of prickly pear plants, which were covered in fruit. It led towards a distant village, the surrounding hills bare and brown. Cutting up through a dirt path to the back of the hotel I walked across a mud-baked field, or so I thought. It turned out to be wet clay. My boots were totally covered in a sticky grey mess.

When I reached the patio, I tried to scrap it off without much success. The cook saw my attempts at cleaning and beckoned me over. He had been hosing down tables on the patio and thought it a good idea to hose my boots too. My trousers and socks were soon soaked, but the clay was remarkably resistant. Exasperated with his efforts the cook broke off a twig from one of the shrubs and told me to scrap the clay off with it and showed me how to turn the hose on and off. He left me for the kitchen. I couldn't remove much of it and in the end took my boots off and left them outside of the door to our room to go into breakfast in my stockinged feet.

Breakfast was almost all you could want. There was bread, cheese, peaches and other fruits plus juices, coffee as well as milk from a large thermos. Giuseppe came over and said that we should follow him after breakfast to our new B&B in the next village. Cicely had already packed the bags and Roger and Linda soon had theirs done too.

Cleaned the dried mud off my boots before getting in your car. Roger followed Giuseppe driving along the road to Rafadal. Passed through a rolling landscape of farms and harvested fields. It wasn't far and soon were at the outskirts of the village. After a roundabout entered a narrow village road that climbed a hill. A short way along it, beyond a small supermarket, Giuseppe stopped at a house. Inside a man and woman all smiles greeted us, but they didn't speak any English. We were shown upstairs to a section of the house separated from the rest by a doorway. Through this was a kitchen breakfast room for the B&B clients and along a corridor from it were rooms. Linda and Roger put their bags in one and I did the same for another. The rooms were pleasant enough and well furnished with a modern en-suite shower room. Giuseppe said we would have dinner at the Reggio Saracena later.

After a short while left Rafadali for the Valley of the Temples, the sky a cobalt blue contrasting with a russet landscape. On arrival parked at the upper car park, near to the Temple of Hera. Although we thought our tickets would be valid again due to our late arrival the previous day we did have to pay again.

Found a number of people already congregating at the ruins. There was not a breath of wind, as we approached the temple of Hera Lacinia to give it its full name. Apparently, newlywed couples, after taking a purifying bath in the nearby River Agrakas, offered Hera Pronuba, the protector of marriage, a ewe lamb that had both its bile and other entrails removed, said to be a symbol of their lasting love.

Access to the temple was restricted by a wire fence. Beyond it stone steps led to the temple platform. Quite a few columns remained intact and I was surprised to discover that at the time of the historian Tommaso Fazello (1490 -1570) the temple was still in a good state. The temple faces east and is the most easterly of all the temples. There are thirteen columns on the north side, but only three of the original six at the front and only a few in parts on the other sides. When the temple was built there were 34 columns in all and the floor plan measured 41.106m by 20.26m with a height of 15.31m. The total floor area is smaller than that of the Zeus temple seen the previous day. Each column consists of four drums with twenty flutes and are 6.32m high with a base diameter of 1.7m and the distance between the columns approximates 1.7m and built in the style of the classical period of Greece. It is dated to between 450 to 440 BCE.

I admired the view looking around the ruins and seeing it with respect to others further down the ridge. It is a pity about the modern viaduct in the far distance that supports a new road to the port for it spoils the whole historic vista of the valley. The viaduct is apparently one of the many illegal building projects carried out by the Mafia for good profit. They have surrounded Agrigento with an appalling unnecessary network of new roads at the expense of the Italian government.

I left the others to walk down to the remains of the Temple of Castor and Pollux to do some sketching. Followed the rocky ridge down towards the Temple of

Concordia we had briefly looked at yesterday. It is of a similar size to Hera, but slightly lower and not the perfect two squares of classical Greece, although it dates from around 430 BCE. In 597 AD the temple was converted to a Christian Basilica.

In 1743 AD the temples of Hera and Concord were declared National Monuments and shortly afterwards in 1784 AD the last remnants of the Christian church buildings were cleared away to reveal the original Greek Temple in its full glory. Today it remains outstanding within an ancient landscape, especially as we experienced under a clear indigo sky with calm blue-green sea below. Its warm golden limestone, like all the other ruins, make it utterly beautiful, although I had heard someone discussing that the original buildings were white having been painted with a mixture of egg white and ground marble, an olden approach to an ersatz cheaper product.

I sat on a ruined wall facing north looking at the remaining columns of the temple of Castor and Pollux. I tried to sketch them, although very bright sunlight with little shadowing offered little help. Only a few people came by when I was there so had the silent place mostly to myself.

Walking on the main pathway I set off back uphill to meet the others at an agreed place and time. I met Cicely by Concordia; she had been photographing around it and found Roger at the exit gate near to Hera. He had been walking along a goat track below the ridge by Hera and told me where Linda was still sketching, or painting. I found her under the shade of trees beneath the temple.

Once we were all gathered together strolled back to the car and drove up to the National Archaeological Museum, its car park nearer to Agrigento. It is built on a site near to some Roman remains and has artefacts set out in well-lit rooms with good labelling, some of which is in English. Within the museum there is also an impressive large-scale model of the temple of Zeus that was informative. In a large room downstairs with high ceilings a telamon was on display. It stood by the staircases situated in the eastern wall at 7.61m tall. The figures, of which there were originally 38, probably represented Atlas, the giant son of Jupiter and Asia. Thirty-eight Telamon, together with columns, supported the temple's huge trabeation.

Also on display were many beautiful artefacts from statues to vases and seal rings. References are made to Akrakas, the original town founded in 581 BCE by colonists from Crete and Rhodes. An archaeological plan showed an urban area of 456 hectares surrounded by a defensive wall 13km long. Although the population of the town was thought to be as much as 800,000 more recent studies and analysis have suggested it was more likely to be no more than 400,000, including slaves and visiting merchants.

An artefact that was illuminating was a pot used for libations. It is decorated with scenes representing the Triquetra, or three legs, or indeed according to its label, the triangular shape of Sicily from which the ancient name of the island is derived. A display of black and red figured vases too was impressive, showing them off to full advantage inside glass cabinets with well-lit shelving. Both the size and artistic decoration amazed us. A few decorative sarcophagi with scenes involving small children gave a touching reminder that these were real people, Greek or Roman, and were like us. Before we left the museum asked at the desk whether we could visit the church, but were told that it was only open for weddings so were not able to see the sarcophagus of Phaedra.

Took a snack lunch at the café and from the terrace viewed the valley of the temples strung out along the ridge below with the sea behind. It was a wondrous, enchanting, magical vision. These memories remain and it was in late 2017 on listening to a programme on the radio about ancient Greeks I recalled the temples in the following poem.

Ancient Greeks

See far away a captivating isle,

Where old ruined Greek temples spread along a ridge,

Skeletal tumbled ruins sleep awhile,

Their past glories retrievable through a time bridge

Back to Magna Graecia in ancient times,

Where towns of southern Sicily flourished,

And bold Akragas flowered in golden climes,

With many classical buildings burnished

It was a fine port that traded widely,

Including Syracuse not far away

Where Archimedes invented wisely,

But Carthaginians were not kept at bay

They sacked the town in 406 BC,

It never recovered its glory days,

But remains of temples look out to sea;

Concordia, Juno, Zeus still amaze

The world of ancient Greeks won't be forgot,

A European priceless heritage;

Sometimes temples stand in a lonely spot,

Sit, search your soul, contemplate, envisage

The day was much hotter, as we set off again heading west along the coast road hoping to discover 'the white cliffs'. We had seen on conceptual art videos back in Palermo about migrant refugees from the Niger. Drove on bypassing the port at Empedocle and headed for Realmonte. Eventually turned off the main coastal road to go down into a network of small lanes towards Capo Rosselo. It wasn't best of areas for it seemed to suffer from unrestricted development, as well as having cement workings.

A lane took us down to a wide flat sandy beach with hardly any people around where we stopped. A bronzed young woman wearing a sarong walked towards us and in the background stark white cliffs with weathered rock shaped in strange flowing patterns met the sand before the sea. Didn't walk to them as Roger wanted to get closer by driving along the shoreline, but unfortunately found no other way to them by road and he decided instead to continue on to the port.

An unknown observer of the white cliffs wrote some time ago, *"The landscape here is among the most stunning with the waters of a crystalline sea on one side and white cliffs on the other. A unique rock formation known as the Scala dei Turchi (Turkish Steps) is a wonderful natural amphitheatre created by erosion, overlooking the sea along the coast of Realmonte, in the province of Agrigento. It is made up of marl, a sedimentary rock consisting of limestone and clay, with a characteristic pure white colour. Scala dei Turchi stands between two sandy beaches and access is from the coast. When you reach the top of the cliff, you are rewarded with a splendid view of Agrigento's coastline. There is also a story that long ago a young couple, Rosa and Peppe, from the village of Realmonte deeply loved each other, but their respective families were opposed to their relationship. Realizing that they could not live apart, the tragic lovers decided to throw themselves from the top of Capo di Monte Rossello. Their bodies, which were never found, rose from the waters transformed into two rocks that are joined together forever."*

We didn't stay long at the port that was without any charm, or interest. However, a little snippet in 'The Eye Witness - Sicily', guidebook about a geological curiosity nearby interested us. It is situated north of Agrigento near to Comitini and is called 'Vulcanlli di Macalube'.

I wanted to navigate Roger on a country road to Favara to get on to the right lanes to the site, but instead Roger being Roger claimed he knew the roads around Agrigento now and said we should take the Palermo road north for a short distance. We drove north looking for a ramp off and took one sign-posted Canicatti and drove into a mess of new roads bearing no resemblance to our map. I indicated to Roger to take a road towards Grotte, then seeing a sign to Aragona directed Roger to turn along the road towards it. The surrounding landscape was wild and desolate steppe and at times we all thought we wouldn't reach our intended destination. Fortunately, after a considerable time saw a rather dilapidated sign directing travelers to Macalube. Followed a country lane seemingly for ages before seeing another sign to give us confidence that we were still on track for this apparent inaccessible curiosity. It was in a countryside of rolling hills with far distant mountains when at last in the distance spied some parked cars that turned out to be the parking place for a visit to Macalube.

A five-minute walk up a dirt track brought us to a large barren site of rolled up dried blue-black mud. At a roped off part saw small glugging eruptions in the mud, as methane gas forced its way through to the surface. This caused micro volcanoes with small wet craters. It was rather similar to cooking with a very thick sauce. At times, it is said, the vulcanelli erupt explosively and emit clay, gas and water together because of a buildup of gas pressure under the surface. However, didn't see this just a small insignificant glugging with gentle pulses every few seconds. The largest vulcanelli seen was a mud hill about a metre tall, but this had no apparent activity. Nevertheless, the site was interesting and was a surprise to us that the mafia hadn't commercially exploited the gas. Left this desolate spot to its glugging and made our way back to our car.

Driving back to Rafadali experienced a wonderful late afternoon light with distant rugged grey-blue peaks set against an intense blue sky. Luminous white cumulus cloud stretched across it. Near to, looked out at a rolling yellow brown landscape of harvested fields smudged here and there with darker areas, as clouds rolled across the sky. Passed through villages, snug in their surroundings, Aragona and S.Elisabetta, until we came at last to Rafadali where in its centre old men sat outside cafés. Lines of chairs faced outward, the sitting men inscrutable, seemingly contented, with the sun painting their lined faces in a golden light. Drew up to another café to sit quietly with a drink before returning to the B&B.

Back in the B&B after resting and showering left for Reggio Sarencena for dinner. The dining room was full but took the table reserved for us and where a good Sicilian red wine waited. A gang of six Americans, including a very large man, sat at a table next to us. They were already eating, tucking in with gusto. Noticed that they had the same fare as we had the day before, but fortunately our menu was changed. The antipasto included something like a Spanish omelet, the primo a gorgeous couscous concoction with pancetta, diced potato and mixed herbs and a main course a juicy grilled pork chop served with a dressed green and red leaved salad. This was followed by a dessert of large bowls of fresh fruit.

After finishing our meal had glasses of limoncello and accompanied mine with a double espresso. Drove back to Rafadali under a bright starry sky. During the night it thundered, the storm carrying on for an hour or two. Couldn't sleep much afterwards for I had turned off the air-conditioning because of the noise it made. In the morning set off to explore more of what Sicily had to offer.

Patio at Reggia Saracena

Sketch of ruins of Temple of Castor & Pollux at Agrigento

Woman in Grecian Dress

Concordia

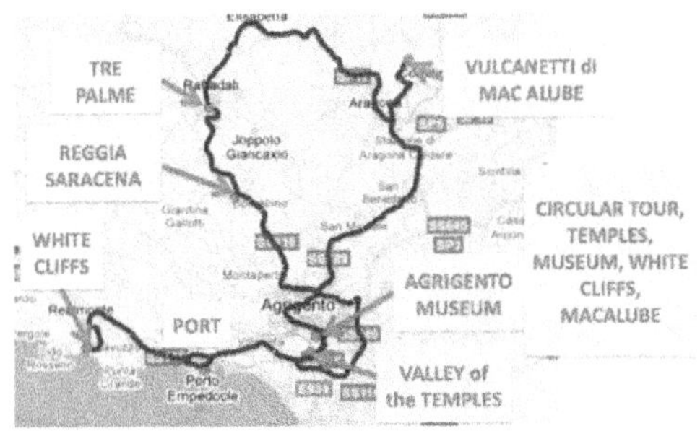

Tours around Agrigento and our two places of accommodation

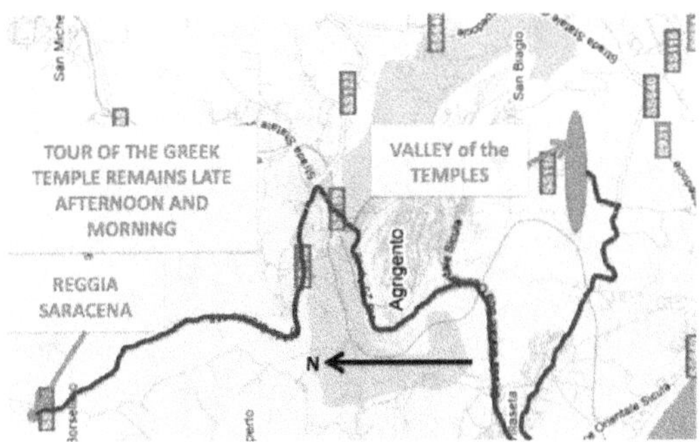

From Reggia Saracena to the Valley of the Temples

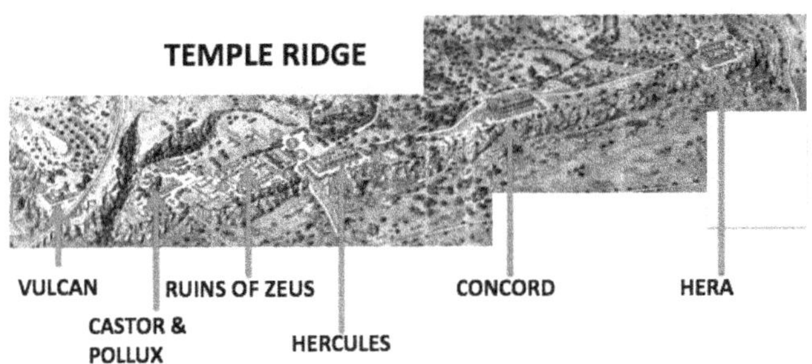

Remains along the ridge at the Valley of the Temples

Sicilian Cart outside of the Valley of Temples

Telamon at the Museum

Looking at Vulcanelli Macalube

Slănic Moldova

Drove fast along the road to Bacău in eastern Romania, a long and tedious drive into the sun. Once within the confines of the large town navigation became difficult. The town is the main industrial centre of Moldavia and provides the largest contribution to the country's GDP. In fact, Bacău's hey day began in the twentieth century when oil was discovered nearby. Under communist rule it became one of the most industrialized regions in the country with two large oil refineries, one at Oneşti and the other at Dărmăneşti.

Road signs left much to be desired for they were not always consistent. For instance, there was a sign to Slănic Moldova just after entering the town, but then not given again for some time; I knew though that we must keep west of the river. I tended to follow the signs to Bucharest for again we had to get onto Route 2 from the north, but at the same time keep in mind it would be only a short distance of travel before turning off it. Although I told Roger to keep to the inside lane, he was impatient and left the lane to pass other vehicles, consequently missed the clearly labelled turn off needed.

It wasn't surprising that Roger got irritated since he had been driving for a long time facing the sun. He thought, quite rightly, I should have picked out the Braşov sign that was the largest town more or less in the direction wanted. Taking the responsibility for navigating as well he turned off the road to Bucharest and followed a van. It took us through a network of narrow town roads to eventually emerge on the right road out of town, Roger is always good following his instincts.

Relaxed again after the hiatus of Bacău and followed the route to Onesti towards the Munţii Vrancei mountains. On reaching Oneşti, which is renowned for its petrochemical industry, skirted most of the town's industrial plants to drive on westward towards Târgu Ocna. This is situated on the left bank of the Trotuş River, a tributary of the Siret River. Târgu Ocna is built on bare hills formed of rock salt situated within the Carpathian Mountains. In fact, the English translation of Ocna is salt mine. The main industry is salt production and is the largest provider in Moldavia. Other industries include wood processing, coal mining, steel producing, and petroleum-based industries.

After leaving Tărgu Ocna behind turned left into the hills along a heavily wooded valley leading towards Slănic Moldova, which was only a few kilometres away. Noted on the way poor looking villages with a few oil derricks standing here and there, as the road continued to take us on up the valley passed by a National Park. Eventually, emerged into a strange collection of buildings. It was the place we were to stay.

****

A complex mixture of faded Belle Époque buildings and communist concrete monstrosities greeted us. The whole place had a feel of mouldering decay, not at all what I had expected. Roger drove through the resort to look for suitable hotels. Perhaps there were good ones, but as it turned out didn't have a chance to find out.

According to tourist literature Slănic-Moldova is well-known and a very beautiful Romanian spa resort that is situated on the eastern slopes, within the foothills of Nemira massifs, of the Eastern Carpathians. Forests of beeches and fir trees surround its location at an elevation of 530m in the valley of the Slănic beck, a tributary of Trotuş River. Unfortunately, descriptions of the place did not tie in with our first impressions. These were '*why are we here*?' but in former times and still probably by Romanians, or Moldavians, it is a resort appreciated for its unique variety of mineral springs, which allegedly through their composition, concentration and complexity have both chemical and therapeutic effects. Its spa potential was developed at the beginning of the nineteenth century and by 1887 became a well-known Spa Town. Our guidebook informed us that the resort has many hotels and villas, a sanatorium complex and various facilities and opportunities for recreation and amusement, concert halls, gaming halls, sports grounds, bowling alley, and a disco. The text goes on to describe the environment as a wild and fascinating landscape that offers the opportunity for short walks in the shady, quiet, narrow valley.

Roger, being impetuous, turned up one of the broken potholed roads that led to a communist looking concrete tower block. A dilapidated structure that looked the worse for wear. I accompanied Roger into a large lobby where a cheery enough man said they had rooms for 50 to 70 lei per night, but only for two nights, as a party of 200 was arriving on Sunday. Didn't take the offer and walked out onto rough crumbling overgrown debris. A couple of worn looking old people sat on a concrete block and stared at us inquisitively. Back in the car found out that the girls didn't like the place and I agreed with them. Going back the way we had come in drove on through the town once more before stopping at the bottom of ascending steps that led up to what looked like a fine 5-star boutique hotel.

After difficult climb up many steep crumbling, dangerous looking, neglected steps to a front door I stopped. A small sign stated 'Private Members Club'. Carefully I backtracked down the steps to the car. Roger drove off once more. There seemed to be nothing around except for not very attractive 2-star hotels and a restaurant, or two. Further on up the road reached the top end of the town where we saw a promising looking place. The Coroana, a 4-star hotel. It has four storeys, the last being within its sloping roof. Moreover, it was freshly painted and looked pleasant enough.

Parked up a rough stony lane between the hotel and what looked to be one of the old communist tower buildings under renovation, or perhaps more correctly being rebuilt in places. It looked awful. A high steel fence surrounded a space at the bottom end of the building site next to the main road. Later learnt that renovation work had been on-going for the last ten years. The reason given was, because the owners had continually run out of money. The part surrounded by the fence was eventually planned to be a swimming pool, but the only workmen seen were working on painting the main building.

Taking the front steps to the Coroana went through the door into reception. There found a jolly well-built man sitting at a desk, by his side a younger man stood military erect in hotel uniform. I discovered that they had two double rooms available for three nights at a price of 50 euros. Told the jolly man that my wife and friends would look at the rooms. Returning to the car the girls said that they would look but make no commitment because they wanted to view other hotels.

The young man in uniform took us up the stairs to show us rooms on the second floor. The rooms looked to be of good size and had en-suite facilities, but as we left one of the rooms spotted Roger scampering up the stairs to the next floor following a rather largish woman. We were quite surprised since he had promised to stay in the car. Following them up to the third floor were shown two more rooms that looked out onto the old communist building, or what was to be the swimming pool. They were pleasant enough with good-looking en-suite facilities, but as with the entire hotel the décor was a little over the top in faux Belle Époque style. Madame hovered near to us saying 'Very Good, Very Good'. She also told us that the room opposite contained a Jacuzzi that we could use. Looking into it saw some kind of tent arrangement that looked like a portable Turkish bath. I didn't think Linda was too keen on this crude looking contraption.

Roger said he didn't like the room at the front and wanted to see one at the side. It was smaller but had a large wardrobe. Of the two rooms Cicely and I liked 301 situated at the front. As we went down the stairs saw

Roger ahead of us shake hands with the jolly man at reception. He had said that we would take the rooms. This was much to the annoyance of the girls. The rooms were 50 euro or 200 lei per night including breakfast. He said that there was no hotel elevator but that he would get one of the boys to take our bags up and he would also move his car so that Roger could park in his place by the fence.

Went up to our rooms again after the bags had been carried up and discovered that both rooms had only one working bedside light and not really a bedside light for it was located half way up the wall. However, the worst for Roger was his shower for it had no fittings to hold the nozzle so he was all for leaving. Calmed him down and sat him on the settee outside of the rooms and eventually he agreed to stay.

Rather than unpacking our bags went down the stairs to the terrace to have a drink calling in at reception to tell them about the lights and to get more pillows. The jolly man said he would attend to it and went on to tell us about the attractions of the area. He recommended a walk up stream to see the various water sources but advised us not to drink from them. There was also a local salt mine to visit and a monastery to see too.

Sat relaxing on the terrace overlooking part of the fencing surrounding the adjacent hotel that was being restored. Painters worked on the wall of the tower block, three of them launching themselves over the side of the roof. Attached by ropes they scrambled down the wall to sit on wooden planks like a swing. Linda thought the activity a little precarious but they did have a safety rope and a harness too. After finishing our welcome cool beers left to walk down through the small quaint town. In fact, at that time a bizarre resort with many buildings requiring maintenance with roads in a shambolic state. Walked through a small park seeing elements of its former grandeur, even though it too was neglected.

A weird atmosphere prevailed. A few, mostly old people, sat on benches with vacant staring eyes. Linda said it was like being on the stage set of *'The Prisoner'*, waiting for something to happen. One or two of the buildings did look in much better shape than the majority and if they were all brought up to that standard the place would come alive. Roger and I went into one of hotels leaving the girls to walk down the road to look at some stalls. Found the hotel much plusher than the one we had booked into and for the same price. Moreover, it had extra facilities like a swimming pool. Roger said, 'Don't tell Linda'. Leaving the hotel didn't walk far and returned to the Coroana a little depressed with its ambiance.

That evening dinner in the hotel was served in a restaurant on the top floor. It turned out to be a miserable affair for the others, but for me OK. I had a starter of mushroom with Gorgonzola cheese followed by a main course of carp cutlet served with tomato salad and frites, both courses I enjoyed, conversely though the dessert was a bit too much. I had ordered the Papanasi with no cream, but when it arrived was served on a large plate with two large donuts plastered with sour cherry jam.   It looked far too much. I ate one of them and left the rest. The others sat with scorn on their faces around a table full of food debris, dried meat, messed up fish and piles of brown potatoes and mushrooms. Yet Roger did finish off with a Finneti, which is like a hazelnut spread on a Pancake. Cicely hardly ate anything at all and wanted a good glass of liqueur to compensate, unfortunately they didn't have one to her liking.

The next day after a good night's sleep woke to a fine sunny morning. Later climbed the stairs to the restaurant to have breakfast. Took a vacant table by a window, a number of people were already eating at other tables. Fetched various things from the help yourself buffet to eat. There was quite a choice to select from with two types of cereal including muesli, various cooked things in trays such as different sausages, fried egg, omelet, as well as salads, tomato, peppers, cheese and bread and jam. The coffee though was inferior being served from an urn. Roger enjoyed himself foraging making up for the previous evening.

After breakfast walked up the attractive wooded valley. A map on a display board by 'the Sources' showed various footpaths. There, saw many people filling up containers with litres of spring water from taps labelled with their water ingredients. It was foul smelling stuff indicating sulphurous products. Followed a footpath along Slănic Beck. The map had showed four stopping points to take the waters but sensibly declined. Chemical stains on rock surfaces over which liquid flowed gave a colourful warning of ingredients.

In the shade of trees further up the valley the footpath diverged away from the stream to become a wider dirt track. Continued walking onwards uphill to emerge eventually from tree cover into full bright sunshine. Many blooming wild flowers added to the pleasant surroundings. During the walk had observed about five different species of butterfly, including a fritillary with a triangular wing formation, and an unknown reddish brown one, Cicely saw a Copper too. We even saw someone drilling for oil in the streambed, or so we thought judging from machinery mounted on a lorry parked beside the track. About half a mile further on passed through the hamlet of Baile Slănic and not long afterwards a cart pulled by two horses came fast towards us. It was piled high with bedding covering cut tree trunks with five lads on board. It passed us by at trotting speed.

I walked back down the hill with Linda, while Roger was with Cicely not too far behind searching out butterflies. Back at the resort walked down through the town to a large Pizza restaurant situated at the end of the park area that was elevated above the main road. Saw a large number of people already eating there. The sides of it open to the elements had flowers in boxes suspended on walls below. Inside ordered pizzas with vinaigrette dressed beetroot and pepper salads plus beer for the four of us.

After lunch drove down the valley to visit the salt mine. It is located in the small town of Tărgu Ocna. Purchased tickets at an office situated within a complex of industrial looking buildings. In a lower area reached by steps a bus stood waiting to take us into the mine. The minibus was almost full but the girls and Roger managed to get seats. I had to stand near to the front. When all was ready the driver got in and drove off to enter a tunnel bored into the hillside. The entrance had dressed stone surrounds and a sign situated over the tunnel arch stating 'Mina Trotus'.

The drive down into the mine was exciting. Drove over a bumpy road surface in a downward spiral, the driver steering on full lock. When it arrived at last within a vast open underground cavern, I was glad to get out of the bus. After everyone had disembarked, we're ushered through a high plastic curtained wall. The air temperature much lower than on the surface, around ten degrees, so put on my fleece. Beyond the curtain entered a large open spacious place that rose to a height of a three-storey house, square cross-sectioned chambers were cut out of the salt off it. Basically, the mine workings were in a grid pattern with equal column dimensions to those of the hollow chambers.

Visited a Church dedicated to St Varvara that was located in the first chamber. It had brightly coloured icons including one that looked like St George killing a dragon but in the shape of an octopus. Splitting up, looked around other chambers separately, but I found there wasn't much else that appealed. In one found a museum, but didn't have enough labels in English to fathom out what it was all about. In another a shop sold masks and painted icons. Discovered in others a five aside football pitch, a basketball court and a kiddies play area. In another part of the mine found a pumped waterfall with a pond below it, in which yellow plastic ducks bobbed around. Strangely in yet another area, coloured plaster Gnomes were positioned incongruously. My thoughts went straight to John Major, British prime minister in the 90's for his brother was famous for selling them, perhaps he had ventured into Romanian territory.

According to the official literature the church built inside a salt dome on level nine was the first underground Orthodox Church in Europe. It is dedicated to St.Varvara because she is known as the miners' protector. It was built during 1992 on the initiative of the mine employees. Positioned at the altar is a set of twenty-four icons, the one on the far left represents St Varvara whilst the far right one represents St. Parascheva, the patron saint of Moldavia. The bishop's throne and the fixtures are all carved out of salt, sculpted by miners, then varnished with some special substance to make them look like wood. The Salt Museum was originally set up inside the salt mine to show the origin and evolution of salt exploitation. It displays some historical, archeological and other sorts of documents and photographs together with collections of mineral samples.

Took a full-length bus back to the surface, I found it comfortable and warm unlike the trip down into the mine. On the drive back up the valley to the Coroana passed by people in fields manually gathering hay into stacks and saw on nearby hills a few rusty oilrigs that didn't seem to be operational.

Reaching the hotel Roger wanted to rest, so I fetched my sketchbook and went down through the park to draw the casino building. It had an elaborate architecture so sat in the sunshine on one of the park benches and started to draw, hoping for peace and quiet.

I found sketching difficult for two main reasons the first being the complex shape and peculiar perspective secondly people were inquisitive. There were many more people out and about, as it was a weekend and on finishing my sketch wasn't too pleased with my effort and thought that I must get an eraser.

Later walking back to the hotel met Cicely who had been taking photographs and went back together. In our room I thought that the towels had been changed but discovered that they hadn't been. Oddly wet towels had been removed from the bathroom and rolled up and placed by our bed. There are many features and practices of the hotel and its staff that are hard to fathom. For example, in the morning, after breakfast, Linda showed me the toilet off the stairs situated just below the top floor, the door to it is about four foot high. Perhaps it is built for children or even midgets. Another quirk that is much more dangerous is an uneven drop of steps on the stairs, some being quite high. This is particularly so for the first step down from floor three. If you don't watch out you can jar your knee. Strangely the stairs to the top floor are made of wood not of marble as the other stairs. This is opposite to the image the hotel wants to give of fake Belle Époque.

Earlier all agreed that we would not risk the hotel restaurant again for dinner and would find an alternative in town. It was seven thirty when we walked down Str Vasile Alecsandri, the highest road in town, to Vila

Teleconstrucţia Hotel. It was supposed to have the best restaurant in town according to the label displayed on its outside, notably it was the same one Roger and myself discovered in the morning, but still kept secret from the girls.

A charming young woman showed us to a table in a fine dining room. It was close to a large circular table that had been set out for a group of children. She said that our meal would be delayed a little, but at the same time brought us some olives, bread and two carafes of Moldavian wine, one white and one red. While waiting a group of thirty children with ages ranging from five to eleven came in with two teachers. They were quiet and orderly and sat down waiting for their meal. A little later meat in gravy with polenta arrived and after a short prayer their meal was served. They ate silently with no disturbance to the rest of the customers in the dining room.

We learnt later from Elena when she came to take our orders that the children were not from an orphanage, as we first thought, but from poor farm worker's families. One or two of the children looked to be very thin, but most seemed to be happy enough. They had been taken on local visits during the day and were staying somewhere nearby. 'World Vision', a Christian charity from the USA, supported the meal and both Roger and I decided to give the teachers 200 lei each to buy the children ice creams for they would only have a one course meal. Gave the money to Elena for her to take to the teachers. They came over to warmly thank us, but could speak no English; Elena though translated for us what they said. Elena had learnt to speak English by first reading comic books, then in school up to eighth grade.

Our first course arrived. It was cheese croquettes served with a tomato salad. For the main course I had the Moldavian Stew that Elena recommended. It contained small pieces of succulent pork, some sausage and pieces of bacon and was served with polenta. It also had a poached egg on top with a scattering of sharp cheese. It was a delicious dish. Linda had chicken livers cooked in red wine and served with green beans and sauté potatoes, Cicely had a filet of perch baked in an almond crust topped with browned flaked almonds and served with a mixture of vegetables and Roger had the same starter as me plus some pork stew served with a Greek salad. During the meal a second sitting of children arrived looking to be from secondary schools. Again, they were well behaved and caused little disturbance in the room. Unfortunately, we didn't know when we gave the money that there would be sixty of them, but perhaps they would just buy ice creams for the young ones

Finally, we indulged in dessert. I had two types of ice cream, Cicely and Linda two Fineti pancakes, and Roger a macaroni cheese. Eventually, Elena came with our bill.

Elena an attractive ethnic Romanian had provided the ambiance and food we wanted. Thanked her wholeheartedly and paid the bill. She and a man, thought to be the manager, came out with us wishing us well for the rest of our holiday. Although our tip had been good it wasn't too large, but I think that they appreciated what we had done for the children, for the hotel had done a lot too. Said that we would return the next day.

By the time we had left the restaurant it was ten thirty and a bright starry sky greeted us, the air temperature still warm and pleasant. Unfortunately, illumination from street lights blocked out most of the stars, which I suspected would be magnificent here with such clear air. Happy after a wonderful meal walked back up to our hotel along an empty silent street. On arrival found the hotel all in darkness. In the jocular mood we were in I said that they had locked us out, but soon discovered that they had. I pressed the bell several times, but nothing happened. Cicely gave Roger a torch for I had found a side door off the terrace that was open. Inside found only a boiler room with no other door. Linda intelligently used her mobile to phone the hotel. The Gauleiter, the wife of the manager, who had tried to persuade us to take the rooms on arrival and who sits at breakfast unsmiling and officious, answered Linda. She said she would be down shortly. After about a minute, lights came on and the door opened. In her nightgown stood Madame in all her full glory. Very annoyed and emotional Linda wanted to know why we had been locked out. In her usual fashion the Gauleiter shrugged this off. "Hotel Full", she said, expressing no apology. Roger said that he would ask for a key in the morning.

Woke early to another fine day with a clear blue sky, the sun yet to illuminate the wooded valley. According to the TV the weather would remain good for at least the next two days. Met up with Linda and Roger at breakfast sitting in our usual place by the window. There were more people in than the previous day and the cook behind the bar looked sternly at me, as I helped myself to most of the muesli. She had to fill up the container again. Later I indulged in an omelet, but it tasted funny, Cicely said that it was probably a dirty pan that it was cooked in. Judging from the cook's repertoire I thought it could be anything from fish to pork, but most probably smoky bacon. It's funny she'd filled a whole container with a mixture of sausage, omelets and bacon. I finished with a piece of marbled cake and had some fresh slices of apple from Linda; the cook kept her eye on me the whole time.

When the Gauleiter came in to the restaurant she just nodded to us; we are now persona non grata. The weather girl on the TV wears a white micro mini and very high heel shoes and struts about, prancing like a new born foal showing off her long legs. A hyperactive little boy with a cap gets away from his mother yet again and rattled some keys he had near to the TV screen. When his cap came off it exposed a shaven head.

As we left the restaurant, The little boy came with us to the door where the stairs fall away steeply, as we left the restaurant. I put my arm out to stop him falling down the stairs, his mother rushed to grab him. She accelerated fast across the floor in a frantic movement with fear in her eyes. She smiled her thanks at me and carried off the struggling lad back to her table for the umpteenth time.

Asked the manager in reception about last night, he apologized saying it wouldn't happen again. His explanation was that the young man on duty had some illness and had to leave the desk, so locked up. I didn't believe him.

Later Roger drove us up the road past the cascade and on along a rough road that wound its way up the mountain twisting and turning through dense woods. In places, the road looked as if at one time it had been cobbled for saw at times old concrete edges appearing amongst the undergrowth. The road was full of potholes and just after another sharp bend became like a rough streamed with boulders and deep ruts. Even Roger thought this to be too difficult to attempt to drive up with our hire car, so he backed up to park off road on a flat grassy area.

Continued walking on up the hill hoping to emerge eventually from the densely packed conifer trees to have a view of the surrounding landscape. In places detected a former pavé road surface. A combination of poor maintenance and bad weather had probably destroyed the original road that was probably further aggravated by heavy forestry cart traffic, and perhaps even lorries. Saw remains of an old stonewall and concrete fixtures that indicated long forgotten barriers; at one time it must have been a good road. Sunbeams, at times, penetrated the dense trees to light up a ridge on the hill ahead, but we never did reach it, or clear the trees. The laborious upward walk became so boring so turned back to the car. Noticed that bird noise was missing, the environment silent and still.

Drove back to the hotel for a ten-minute break before driving on down to the Vila Teleconstrucția. Elena greeted us and said for us to go into the dining room and to sit at one of the tables. Told her that we wanted to eat there in the evening and she gave us the menu to look at. She was smartly dressed in a decorative white cotton blouse designed with sown over panels in both chevron and vertical stripes. It also had a round neck and short sleeves presenting a highly fashionable look. She also wore a black wrap around skirt laced up on the left side showing a bare leg to the thigh and wore dangly gold earrings and black high heel shoes to finish off the whole effect. Her long hair was pulled back into a plated single pigtail that fell to her waist. She said that I could take a photograph and smiled at me with pleasure.

I chose the perch in wine sauce with green beans. Cicely chose a chicken dish with honey and in discussion with Elena found out that there would be a side dish of special wild mushrooms. These were in season and foraged from the surrounding woods. She told us that we could have it as a starter. Roger ordered some pork dish and Linda baked perch with vegetables. After she had taken our orders for the main course, she said to follow her, as she would show us the indoor swimming pool. It was large and Linda said she would like to try it out, Elena said we were all welcome to do so. On leaving thanked her saying we would be there at seven thirty in the evening.

It was hot outside and got into our car to drive down towards Tărgu Ocna. On the way hoped to find a road to the monastery shown on our map, but the map showed no road. Yet, after entering the small village of Cerdac a brown road sign indicated the Monastery of Stefan cel Mare to our right.

Drove along this narrow road that soon deteriorated into a rough stony track. It steeply ascended the hillside behind the village. Higher up the state of the track worsened, with the Monastery still 6km away. Drove on through areas of birch trees and open land giving us a panoramic landscape and good views of both the valley and mountains beyond. Back up the valley, towards Slanic, distant mountain peaks changed from blue to light grey to fade into the sky.

After passing a hill farm saw other vehicles coming down the hillside towards us. They were mainly 4X4's and shortly afterwards saw the monastery, partially obscured by trees, on a distant ridge. The road looped around the hillside until it came to a fork. I thought we should drive straight on up towards the satellite repeater station, seen above us, but Linda disagreed and said to take the left fork. After going 100m further on, Roger stopped, he thought the road wasn't right. It looked to him to be curving around the hillside to eventually drop back down into the valley.

I got out of the car and recced where the road was going by climbing up a bank to a plateau area where I found the remains of a capped off oilrig. To my right, further up the hill, saw the tops of the monastery building complex, my original route at the fork was right. Back at the car Roger wasn't satisfied with this conclusion so went out a second time to go beyond the plateau area further along the road and saw a working oil derrick close up and yet another further along the road with a donkey pump. The road continued on past this with no signs of a road turning up the hill to the right and presumed that the road would eventually descend into the valley far below. I walked back to the car where the others stood looking at the beautiful surroundings.

Drove back to the fork where another car was on its way and let it pass before turning up to the monastery. Parked the car outside of the complex near to a gateway. The monastery looked newly built and well looked after and by the gate, in a fenced off paddock, a brown horse rubbed its head on a wooden post rail. The site provided a glorious view of the wooded valley and Carpathians beyond.

The white walled gateway had three small towers their tops finished off with a witch's hat finish using red-brown tiles. Followed Roger through the arched entrance into a stone walled enclosure. From there a stone slab pathway led up a rise flanked by low stone walls topped at intervals with stone pillars connected by three wooden rails. They were bordered on the other side with flowering roses and very short cypress trees.

Roger mounted marble steps up to a small white walled church to go inside, while I looked around outside. The church had white rendered walls over a bare stone base and mounted on its overhanging tiled roof was a tower. It was built in two tiers and finished off in the shape of a witch's hat. Saw other buildings situated within the walls of the complex and a large one beyond the church looked like living quarters. Many flowers decorated its surrounding garden. Had good feelings especially with an intense indigo sky and sunshine reflecting off the brilliant white surfaces of buildings.

The Monastery was founded in 1999 by Vasile Gavrila. Later in 2003, construction of the church started. On the Feast of Saint Stephen in 2006 the Great Slănic Monastery was completed and the church consecrated.

I followed Roger up the steps to the church noticing above the doorway three new frescos painted in the old style. Inside were three rooms with all walls covered in brightly coloured frescos. They were painted in traditional Byzantine style, similar to previous churches visited in Romania. In addition to this were images of two abbots. There is also an icon of Stefan cel Mare in silver to be seen. A ceiling painting under the tower octagon portrayed Christ Pantokrator.

Roger had been investigating what was behind a screen when I turned on instinct to find standing behind me a young bearded monk. He had no hat and his long flowing hair was tied back in a ponytail. He didn't speak any English so I continued taking photographs of the images not wanting to stop and afterwards moved back towards the entrance followed by the monk. St Stephan's emblem was over the doorway into room two and I gave the monk 10 lei, which he seemed pleased with.

Having seen enough went back outside into the sunshine followed by the monk. Roger tried to converse with him asking if there was another way down to the valley. He had some words of English and indicated that the quickest way down was past the oil derricks. It was only

3km travel but the first 1km was extremely rough and very difficult to drive along. After expressing our thanks to the monk, he left for his quarters while we took the path back to the gate and the car.

Sensibly Roger decided to drive back down the way we had come in. Found it much easier going down and were soon at the Slănic road where we turned left to drive back to the hotel. On arrival in town found many more tourists around than on previous days so Roger had to find a new place to park the car.

The hotel didn't do lunches in the bar area so walked down to the pizza restaurant. The place was very busy, nevertheless got a table and ordered two pizzas, a cabbage salad, three beers and a lemon tea for Cicely. After lunch Roger went back to the hotel to rest and read a book, while Linda and Cicely said they wanted to do some shopping at a supermarket so I took my backpack with my sketchbook and pencils to sit on a bench on the bankside overlooking a domed grandstand.

I found it a little hot sitting in the full sun, but was loth to leave. The density of people going past me was much less than the previous day and didn't bother me. But felt I was getting worse sketching with my long distant glasses on, it just doesn't work. Cicely came by to visit and asked me when I was going back to the hotel, I said about five. Linda apparently had gone back to the hotel after shopping, I discovered later that she had gone swimming in the pool at Elena's place. The time went on and my sketching didn't improve so went back up towards the hotel and came across Cicely photographing butterflies in a meadow.

We walked back together to the hotel and our room. The bedding had been changed, but arranged in their peculiar fashion. It didn't take us long to change it to how we liked it, such a strange eccentric hotel.

Later walked down to the Vila Teleconstrucția in a warm evening. On arrival Elena greeted us. She smiled happily before showing us to our table. I ordered a starter of pickled fungus and some potato wedges to go with my perch dish in wine sauce served with fine green beans, also ordered the Papanasi for dessert. It is made with a cottage cheese filling.

With the starters Elena brought to us a small carafe of bilberry liqueur with four small glasses. The starters included some mashed cooked vegetables, like a ratatouille mix. In conversation I asked Elena whether she could recommend any hotels in Bucharest, on hearing this her partner began looking on the Web from his laptop.

The meal was excellent and during it Elena's partner had looked through many hotel options and called Roger over a few times to look at them and get his advice. He eventually homed in on one called Hotel Unique and before dessert arrived called us both over to look at it. Afterwards agreed to go ahead with booking it on line and were given a printout copy. They both had been extremely helpful to us so tipped them well, as the meal and the service had been excellent too.

Before leaving Elena and her partner wished us well and presented us with two bottles of a local wine. Elena kissed us and her partner shook our hands gratefully then waved goodbye from the top of the steps. Strolling back up to our hotel saw two young men from the hotel who had previously helped us out. It was their evening off and they looked like they were dressed to kill. They were going to dance at the Casino disco. On our way to dinner saw many girls entering the place dressed in their glad rags.

At the hotel the manager was on duty and wished us goodnight. Situated on our landing area a young couple sat happily on a settee drinking wine. Fortunately, their baby was asleep on their balcony. They told us they were from Bucharest and had just started their holiday. They had found the hotel through the Web. They too thought Slănic strange but were only staying for a couple of days before they would head north.

Next day the morning was fine and sunny. At breakfast found a different chef on duty, a male one who was much more pleasant and prepared good scrambled eggs for us. After breakfast paid our bill at reception, 714 lei for three nights and one dinner and said our goodbyes to the maid before leaving. The manager gave us a hotel card after we gave our thanks and said goodbye to him. Perhaps he hoped recommendations would be forthcoming.

It had been an experience visiting Slănic, some good some bad in a way though the good exceeded the bad. It was nine twenty when Roger drove off down the secluded valley leaving Slănic far behind going on through

Onesti to the wider Siret Valley. Eventually reached National Highway, E85, at Adjud. This city, situated on the plain is surrounded by hills up to a height of 400m located at the foot of the Southern Carpathians. We were now on route to Bucharest for rather different experiences

Slănic Beck

Cart with logs near to Baile Slănic

Entrance to Salt Mine

Casino at Slănic-Moldova

Sketching in the Park

Holiday in the Park at Slănic-Moldova

Elena at Vila Teleconstrucţia

Roger and the Monk at Monastery of Stefan cel Mare

Sketch of Band Stand Slănic-Moldova

Alesia

It was our last morning in mid-August of 1984. Had been staying at the Hotel de la Poste in Saulieu, which is situated in the Côte-d'Or, a department in the Bourgogne-Franche-Comté region in eastern France. Dense fog didn't deter me from a run of about thirty minutes in the surrounding countryside before I returned to pack the car. Our room with its thick carpeted walls and ceiling had certainly been a surprise and awful to live in. A little later took our last breakfast there before checking out of the hotel. Found no croissants available just bread and buns. A coach party of tourists that had arrived the previous evening had left early consuming the lot. Saying our goodbyes drove off in the direction of Semur en Auxois with fog still holding fast. Our offside front light was not working due to the earlier accident and had to take great care whilst driving and also avoid the notice of police for we had no way of getting it repaired in time.

Fortunately, arrived safely in Semur under a dull grey sky, the fog had completely dispersed. Old Semur is located in an elevated position and built on underlying rose granite. The l'Armançon river almost surrounds it. Centuries ago, the waters were fast flowing but after a dam was built upstream in the nineteenth-century they became sluggish. Yet the town today is still almost surrounded by its old ramparts, though parts are plainly poorly maintained. Fortifications were first built in the One Hundred Years War, when the Dukes of Burgundy fought on the side of the English. Two conical hat towers form part of a more recent entrance gate that is situated near to a sixteenth century bridge. Left the parked car to walk over and look at one of the towers. Found its masonry badly cracked from top to bottom.

Our walk took us both along the high ramparts as well as along the bottom of the walls. Admired the well looked after vegetable gardens between the road and river and noticed that the shallow river was widely covered by lily pads. It must be a picture when in flower. Just after an old watermill, had good views from ancient bridge of the town and river and later on from the Sixteenth Century Bridge.

Strolled up into the town via a passage adjacent to one of the towers before turning left up an uneven cobbled lane. It was badly in need of repair and lined with agéd medieval houses. To our right saw, closed off, many other ancient alleys. They were probably now part of private property. By one such alleyway an old wattle and daub timber framed house had a second storey projecting out over the lane. Visited a church, which looked very tatty on the outside but in the end proved worth a visit. It had some old stained glass as well as two modern windows. These latter windows portrayed the Great War of 1914-1918 and remembrance to Americans in the war of 1939-1945. Left the church to go further into town then later to pass through an ancient town gate to walk back to the car.

While driving out of Semur toward the village of Lantilly a change in the weather for the better improved our spirits.

Just outside of the village turned towards Alise St Reine. It is located high above the village of Les Laumes. After driving up the hill to it parked next to the church.

Sunshine had broken through the cloud cover, as we walked up a steep hill towards the ancient town of Alesia, a Gallic oppidum, which lay at the foot of Mont Auxois

French children are taught in history lessons at school about their Celtic heritage and the Gallic wars against the Romans. These eventually ended in defeat of Gaul by the armies of Julia Caesar. In particular they learn the story of Vercingetorix and Alesia.

The story goes, around 59 BCE, Rome through Julius Caesar set out to supress major uprisings in Gaul. During the next seven years two military campaigns were fought as he tried to pacify the various Celtic tribes. It was in 52 BCE that Vercingetorix of the Arveni tribe who rallied together a number of other tribes to fight back with strength. Caesar meanwhile had sacked the major city of Avaricum, which in future years became Bourges, that was home to the Bituriges, a powerful tribe. Later Caesar feeling very confident tried to take a hill fort controlled by the Arverni called Gergovia. The place is near to the modern town of Clemont Ferrand, but he was forced to retreat. The Gauls, under the command of Vercingetorix had set up a strong defensive position. Cutting his losses Caesar left to march south with his army of ten legions to a region of today's north west Italy. Once there he increased his army to sixty thousand men with ten thousand reserves from Germania.

During the time that Caesar was away the Gallic tribes met at one of the most important hill forts in Gaul, Bibracte, now the modern town of Mont Beuvray in Burgundy. Most tribes were represented with the exception of three. They elected Vercingetorix as general of their unified forces.

In the summer of 52 BCE there were several skirmishes between Caesar's cavalry and that of the Gauls, finally the Gauls we thoroughly routed. Vercingetorix decided the time was not ripe for a final pitched battle and retreated with his remaining force of eighty thousand men to the hill fort of Alesia that belonged to the Mandubii tribe.

It was at Alesia that the final outcome of the Gallic wars would be realized. It was a strong position surrounded by river valleys. Caesar surmising how many men Vercingetorix must have and in addition taking account of the normal population of the hill fort decided to lay siege. He thought that it wouldn't take too long for starvation to develop. So, he commanded his men to construct a circumvallation, that is fortifications to surround Alesia. Vercingetorix seeing this sent out cavalry to get provisions, as he had only about a month's worth of supplies. Also, at the same time try to destroy and prevent the building of further aggressive fortifications. Caesar's Germanic cavalry though kept them from doing any serious damage. During the fracas a number of Gallic cavalry managed to escape the defensive ring. Caesar seeing this expected a relief force to be sent and ordered a contravallation, that is a second set of fortifications facing outwards and kept his army between the two lines of encircling forts. The details of this engineering work are known from Caesar's *Commentaries* and archaeological excavations on the site. Vercingetorix's cavalry continually raided the construction works attempting to prevent a full enclosure, but the Germanic auxiliary cavalry proved its value to Caesar and kept the raiders at bay.

The second line was identical to the first in design and extended for 21 kilometres, including four cavalry camps. This set of fortifications was to protect the Roman army when the relief Gallic forces arrived, as they were besiegers preparing to be besieged.

The living conditions in Alesia became increasingly worse. Too many people were crowded inside the plateau fortifications competing for too little food. A crunch point came and the Mandubii decided to save food for Vercingetorix's men and expel their women and children from the citadel. They hoped that Caesar would open a breach in fortifications and let them go but Caesar did not instead he issued orders that nothing should be done and the civilians were left to starve in the no man's land between the city walls and the circumvallation. Seeing what had happened caused the Mandubii inside the citadel to lose their optimism and self-esteem.

The Gallic cavalry that had escaped managed to the Gallic tribes and secure a relief force of 250,000 men. It was commanded by four generals from four tribes plus Vercassivellaunus of the Arvernii. But in the mean time Vercingetorix was battling to keep spirits up. He had faced the threat of surrender by some of his men, but the relief force arrived in his desperate hour. This change of circumstances strengthened the resolve of the besieged to resist and fight for another day.

The relief force set up camp a short distance from Caesar's outer fortifications. Alesia's defenders looked out at them from their hilltop and prepared for an attack. The following day, a battle commenced between the three armies. It raged all day and went into a second day of hard fighting. In the end the relief force suffered heavy losses at the defensive and siege fortifications and had to retreat. Seeing this Alesia's defenders had to retreat once more to the confines of the hill fort.

When the third day dawned Gallic scouts from the relief force spotted a gap in the outer defences due to the topology of a steep hill. Vercassivellaunus saw an opportunity and led 60,000 Gauls through the gap and overcame the Roman fortifications. At the same time, Vercingetorix's soldiers attempted to force their way over the inner wall on all sides. Caesar realizing the critical stage of battle led four cohorts and directed cavalry to go around the outer wall and attack Vercassivellaunus's forces from behind. The Roman cavalry managed to cut them down and captured Vercassivellaunus. The defenders in the citadel saw the disaster from high up and called their soldiers back from the field. Some of the Gallic relief force who survived at the outer defensive wall returned to their camp and fled the field with any remaining troops. That night the Roman cavalry attacked their rear, killing or capturing most of these fleeing Gallic warriors.

Vercingetorix convened a meeting with Gallic leaders in the citadel to decide what to do next considering their precarious position. The next day envoys were sent out to Caesar and he instructed them to surrender and lay down their arms. Later the tribal chieftains capitulated meeting Caesar at the front of his camp to surrender Alesia to him and lay down their arms. They also delivered Vercingetorix for his further instructions. Caesar sent him to Rome in chains together with other Gallic captives, assigning one to each to his remaining soldiers as slaves. It wasn't the end of the war with Gaul, but the battle for Alesia was the last major conflict. It took two further summers to eliminate the final resistance.

The Senate in Rome honoured Caesar with much praise and ceremony for bringing Gaul into the Roman republic and over time the whereabouts of Alesia was lost.

Centuries later, during the period of Napoleon III, Alise-Sainte-Reine was declared the site of Alesia. The emperor wanted a unifying spirit for France and recognised that the story of Vercingetorix would be a boost to morale, for it was he who forged the first pan alliance of Gallic tribes. As a consequence, a monumental and romantic statue representing the Gallic leader was erected on a hilltop where the ancient site of Alesia was thought to be.

Many historians doubted the truth of Napoleon's diktat and thought his motives were political, even though archaeological evidence seemed to support the claim. Historical disputes took a dramatic turn after World War Two when André Berthier, an archaeologist and archivist, presented new evidence. After extensive studies, from

Caesars written work, and field work in the Jura declared the site of Alesia to be Chaux-des-Crotenay in a published book. His conclusions were a better fit with historical record. Danielle Door a professor of history at the Sorbonne backed this conclusion. But the debate goes on and Franco-German excavations at Alise in the 1990's seemed to confirm the original choice for the site of Alesia.

Whatever the truth of the arguments this quiet backwater is now at peace. Walked downhill to the village, seeing its red topped roofs below us and beyond them green wooded hills masked in mist. In a cornfield in which catch crops of potatoes and turnips grew between the rows an old man leisurely gathered harvested potatoes and placed them into a large plastic bin. At the main village road turned right and after a short while turned right again to a steep road leading to a viewing point.

The imposing large statue, representing Vercingetorix stood there. It showed him looking out to the west. Steep wooden steps led down to the village and as we walked down went by a house with double pink hollyhock growing outside. Wild parsley too grew profusely at the edge of the path. At the bottom turned left to climb up through the village back towards the car.

On our way, bought a half baguette from a Boulangerie for lunch as it was nearing noon. In a quiet small square at a cross roads had good views of the valley beyond. A statue of Joan d'Arc, very much like the on erected in

Paris., stood there, another local hero labelled 'Joan d'Arc de Bourgogne'.

Cracked Tower at Semur en Auxois

Town Gate at Semur en Auxois

Statue Representing Vercingetorix at Alesia

Walking Back to the Village of Alise St Reine